DESPERATELY SEEKING PURPOSE

Why Am I Here?

**Each Generations' Role
in Raising Global Consciousness**

BY MAXINE JONES

DESPERATELY SEEKING PURPOSE

Cherry Tree Publishing
PO Box 450962
Atlanta, Georgia 31145
www.cherrytreepublishing.com

**CHERRY TREE
PUBLISHING, INC.**

ISBN 978-0-9797841-1-8

Library of Congress Control Number: TXu1-356-027

Printed in the United States of America

Editing by Diane Sears, DiVerse Media LLC, www.di-verse-media.com

Cover design and inside layout by Jill Shargaa, Shargaa Illustration & Design, www.shargaa.com

Author photograph by Keri Greenberg

To order the book, please visit www.maxinejonesandassociates.com

The publisher offers discounts on this book when ordered in quantity. Please contact Cherry Tree Publishing at info@cherrytreepublishing.com

Other books by Maxine Jones

Stretch Your Wings and Fly Collection

Meet Your Soul: Stretch Your Wings and Fly
Connecting with Your Quantum Power

Launch Your Inner Radar: Empowering Your Soul
A Guide to Activating Your Life Purpose

Take the Limits Off Your Power: Freeing Your Hidden Success
A Guide to Feeding Your Hungry Soul

Soul Relationships: Mates, Partners and Teams
A Guide to Creating a Life with Greater Purpose

DESPERATELY SEEKING PURPOSE

DEDICATION

This book is dedicated to my co-creation partners and teams. It took me 30 years, eight months and 17days to bring to life.

My clients finally got through to me that the answer "You are your purpose" was not enough. They wouldn't accept that finding purpose would happen naturally if they lived their potential. They wanted steps to take to get there.

"We're ready to express the magnificence you tell us we are as human beings, the magnificence we know we embody," they told me. "As we embrace all that we came to this life to be, we're ready for direction, clarity, support and action."

This book helps people move the seeds of their possibility into the soil that will support their growth and help them develop into all they can be. I've discovered along the way that everyone is here in this life contributing a unique expression of a grand global purpose, manifesting the magnificence and possibility of our united human greatness.

Thank you for prodding me along and encouraging me to incubate the seeds.

TABLE OF
CONTENTS

Have you ever sensed you're supposed to be doing something bigger with your life?
- ❏ Signs you're ready to explore purpose
- ❏ Signs purpose is breaking through
- • Dual Realities
    - ❏ Living in the demands of 2 realities – daily world and ideal world
- • The Search

How do you feel about purpose?
- • Purpose Questionnaire
- • How Others Responded:
    - ❏ The concept of purpose
    - ❏ Searching for purpose
    - ❏ Frustration

THE JOURNEY OF HUMANITY IS THE JOURNEY
FROM IGNORANCE TO ENLIGHTENMENT.

– DENG MING-DAO

ALL TRUTH PASSES THROUGH THREE STAGES:
FIRST, IT IS RIDICULED; SECOND, IT IS VIOLENTLY
OPPOSED; THIRD, IT IS ACCEPTED AS BEING SELF-
EVIDENT.

– ARTHUR SHOPENHAUER

IF YOU WOULD BE A REAL SEEKER AFTER TRUTH,
IT IS NECESSARY THAT AT LEAST ONCE IN YOUR LIFE,
YOU DOUBT, AS FAR AS POSSIBLE, ALL THINGS.

– RENE DESCARTES

INTRODUCTION

I was sitting with a group of my colleagues and peers, and the conversation moved from light to philosophical. It was the standard appraisal of the world, human advancement and possibilities – the ongoing hopeful and grand debate of the planet, humanity, our environment and technology and, of course, the staying power and value of politics, religion and economics. We weighed the potentials and talked about how to solve all of the world's problems.

Then the conversation turned from philosophical to real.

One participant invited us to open doors within ourselves and reveal our personal truth. He made the statement, "That was fun, and I feel alive and part of a grand life again. But after I leave this room, and two or three days from now, then what? What does it all really mean? What have we really done? What is it all about?"

We looked around the room at each other, savoring the connection of the moment, and he continued.

"I'm not sure how I really fit into the big picture. What am I doing? Nothing, and I know I have a responsibility. I know I can make a real contribution, but I don't know where to start. Am I missing something? I'm not stupid. I just don't get it. How about you?" He looked around at each of us. "Does anyone know what it's all really about? What's your purpose? What's our purpose?"

I can't say I was surprised at what I was hearing, nor was it anything new. But this time something about the context and setting struck me differently. I listened, and I heard real questions, concerns and frustrations. The conversation became personal, even private.

I heard a tone of urgency that was not simply ranting or observation or debate, but a real desire, a sincere need, a clear intention to do something, to find resolution to a question that didn't have an answer. The people in this room were looking for a genuine power to get engaged in a new way. Their constructive dialogue had ignited a real awareness that exposed a raw truth and honesty, and it was more universal than individual.

When it comes to examining purpose, I've heard people use the words "empty," "unfulfilled," "on the wrong track," "disappointed." Their deep expressions of personal pain, sadness and confusion come from reaching yet another unexplained dead end. They seem to come to a place where thinking is just not enough, and where feeling takes them in another endless circle.

But I've also heard "excited" and "exhilarated" come up again and again. Somehow this exploration is fulfilling, even when it doesn't seem to be fruitful. Simply having the sense that there is something greater in each of us seems to set off an inner spark that races through us, igniting the remembrance of personal convictions and passion about what life can be.

After that evening's conversation with my peers, I came away with a personal realization and deeper understanding of why I needed to write this book. This is about the real stuff that comes out of our personal knowing and truth – the things we don't often talk about with ourselves, let alone a bunch of strangers and, even more importantly, our colleagues and peers. This is the stuff we talk about in a client or patient relationship, or with our best and most confidential friend, but not out in the open, raw, uncensored and vulnerable in public.

I was deeply moved, as we all were. We had touched on something important and big for all of us, a deeper, more real truth.

It was expressed, it was out there on the table, and we couldn't take any of it back.

I wondered, Why can't I have this kind of connection and communication more often? Where do people talk these days? Why can't life be this real? These questions led to more questions that led to this book.

An encoded seed lies within each of us, and it contains a map of our united life purpose. Whether we've awakened to it yet or not, we were born with something enormous and strong inside us that cannot be ignored. It ignites the mysterious inner drive that activates hope and inspiration, pushing us, waking up our passion to be more and to do more with our life.

That purpose is undeniable. It's global. It's individual, yet it's not recognizable when expressed alone. It needs others – their vision, their piece – and bit by bit, the vision starts to be revealed, gaining strength through recognition.

One of our deepest fears is that we'll look back and wonder why we didn't have the guts to do something of real value with our lives.

It's time to write this story, our story, the story of all generations seeking a purpose that unites us. We've gained momentum since the 1970s, when we knew we had a purpose but weren't ready to fulfill it yet. The seeds inside us are about to blossom. The flower power is strong and alive, ready for the next step on its mission.

OUR DEEPEST FEAR IS NOT THAT WE ARE INADEQUATE. OUR DEEPEST FEAR IS THAT WE ARE POWERFUL BEYOND MEASURE. IT IS OUR LIGHT, NOT OUR DARKNESS, THAT MOST FRIGHTENS US. WE ASK OURSELVES, WHO AM I TO BE BRILLIANT, GORGEOUS, TALENTED, FABULOUS? ACTUALLY, WHO ARE YOU NOT TO BE? YOU ARE A CHILD OF GOD. YOUR PLAYING SMALL DOES NOT SERVE THE WORLD. THERE IS NOTHING ENLIGHTENED ABOUT SHRINKING SO THAT OTHER PEOPLE WON'T FEEL INSECURE AROUND YOU. WE ARE ALL MEANT TO SHINE, AS CHILDREN DO. WE WERE BORN TO MAKE MANIFEST THE GLORY OF GOD THAT IS WITHIN US. IT'S NOT JUST IN SOME OF US; IT'S IN EVERYONE. AND AS WE LET OUR OWN LIGHT SHINE, WE UNCONSCIOUSLY GIVE OTHER PEOPLE PERMISSION TO DO THE SAME. AS WE ARE LIBERATED FROM OUR OWN FEAR, OUR PRESENCE AUTOMATICALLY LIBERATES OTHERS.

– MARIANNE WILLIAMSON

CHAPTER 1

SOMETHING BIGGER

Have you ever sensed you're supposed to be doing something bigger with your life?

Consider this question against the backdrop of what's happening in the world today. We're seeing both extremes: the very worst expression of humanity, with war and all its scary, ugly sides, alongside development of magnificent projects that involve profound technology and sweeping humanitarian efforts.

It's a time when geeks turn genius, when going from rags to riches is commonplace. It's a time of creative renaissance in books, art, music and language, with personal expression and truth erupting from every possible crack and crevice.

It's an extraordinary time to be alive – or to awaken, become aware and evolve. This undercurrent of life gives us the impetus to test whether we really matter. Could it be true that one individual among billions has value as a piece of the whole, and that without that person's tiny contribution, the creation is left unfinished?

It's not enough to spend one's whole life on personal survival instead of seeking awareness of the bigger picture. Doing so is a tragic under-use of life. It borders on being irresponsible.

Yet most of us continue to focus on daily minutiae. Our time, resources, thoughts and emotions are besieged by life's demand

Signs you're ready to explore purpose

- You feel empty, unfulfilled, frustrated, urgent, uncomfortable, unclear.
- Mundane tasks eat up your time.
- You wonder whether you're supposed to be doing something else, but you're afraid to say that out loud.
- You ask yourself, "Am I the only one who doesn't get it?" or "Am I crazy?"
- You sense you don't fit in the mold.
- You feel like you have a secret you're hesitant to share.
- Questions haunt you and you're not sure why.
- You have the trappings of success but not the satisfaction.

for our immediate, undivided attention. And before we know it, another birthday has come and gone. The big events fade into the recesses of our minds as we're swept into the next daily crisis.

In the middle of it all, we catch glimpses of a bigger picture. This feeling that there's something more gives us hope about the possibility and power that exist in our deepest beings to explore, discover and fulfill. Ever-present within us, like a seed, our hope embodies the encoded message of who we are and what we're here to do, to be, to feel and to know about ourselves and our world.

Our sense of greater purpose exists unscathed, undiluted and unencumbered by life's demands that bombard us in every moment of our existence. When we can break through everyday survival mode – during times when we feel good about ourselves, when life is moving forward and making sense – then we begin to focus on the bigger picture. That's when we contemplate greater purpose.

Sometimes this sense breaks through its boundary, past the protection that encapsulates it, and stirs our curiosity, cracking open the seed, causing it to release some of our deepest wisdom into our awareness. At that moment, when that sense breaks through into our conscious mind, the way we see ourselves and our lives changes. Even if it's only for that moment, the impact can be overwhelming, profound and unforgettable.

The reaction to this sense of awareness varies from person to person, but we all feel its unmistakable presence. It's undeniable and hard to push away. It grabs us, haunts us for days, and exposes a part of who we are, if only for an instant.

Signs purpose is breaking through

- High achievement, social service, religious devotion and spiritual searching are not yielding answers.
- You say to yourself, "I want more. I am more. There has to be something more."
- Glimpses of purpose seem too lofty, "pie in the sky," impractical and beyond reach when you think about them logically.
- You're saying, "I'm not stupid, but I'm not getting it."

Some of our greatest innovations and creations have come out of those tiny moments when life's purpose rises to the surface just enough to inspire, direct and spur us into action.

Look around. New expression is exploding. This is a time of accelerated technological advancement that renders today's newest, greatest, most profound discoveries obsolete within 90 days of their introduction. It's a time when modern medical science threatens to create a better, more perfect human being, telling us reproduction and procreation are outdated.

On the internet, our children are revealing intimate things about themselves to total strangers around the world that we would never have dreamed of discussing with our closest friends and family members. They have more to say, to be, to explore and to create than we ever knew was possible. They share a unified vision of greater possibility and potential. The geographic, religious, political, cultural, socioeconomic status we've dedicated generations of resources and precious life to protect and defend are simply wiped away by the click of a mouse.

In their innocence and trust, they are uplifting humanity. We fear if we don't find a way to get on board, we'll be left behind, unfulfilled and lost.

DUAL REALITIES

The greatness we hold so deeply inside is our seed of potential and purpose. When the environment and circumstances are just right, that seed begins to stir something within us.

I've noticed this stirring grow more frequent in many people since the change of the millennium, arousing our awareness. Its provocation is getting stronger, and the effect lasting longer. It's having an impact in a way that noticeably consumes time, distracts the mind, agitates our emotions and revs up our passion.

All of this inner uproar overshadows our mundane and immediate life chores, causing us to become distracted, irrational and Illogical. The mind starts to reprioritize life.

It's like being in love. Something takes over our sanity and we're lost in the mysterious power we get from having a sense of purpose. It stimulates hope, and our wildest dreams take on new life. Our imaginations run wild, our hearts open, and the power of possibility takes over our sense and sensibility.

Finding purpose used to be a life quest we contemplated if and when we had the luxury of time and energy. Today, it's become a drive, a race, a question that haunts us, causing us to wake up and challenge ourselves to take action. It demands that we be more, messing with our hearts and minds, disturbing our peace, interfering with our pleasure. It keeps us from settling into the bliss of contentment and safety of the mundane.

We live in a dual world – one our children don't know yet – that causes us to seek. One reality fades out and the other takes over, sometimes in a flash, sometimes ever so gradually.

This reality shifting is born out of the duality of physical reality often described as the roller coaster of life. The greatness we hold inside, and the demands and responsibility that consume us on the outside, set us up each day to cope with the excruciating dilemma of the two worlds expressing themselves simultaneously.

The inner reality is alive, and it drives itself into the light of our awareness. It's looking for support and acknowledgement to give it strength and expression. This inner drive is unique to each of us. It's part of what makes us human. However, its expression makes it individual. It's personal – that's what makes it so fun, as well as confusing and scary. There is room for every human seed to be fully expressed.

This parallel inner world is an alternative way. It's not about rebellion or resistance or anarchy, it's about possibility that can exist alongside the external forces of survival and demand. It's not about changing, it's about adding and adding and adding until living our purpose becomes a choice, an option, an alternative.

As we experience this dual reality, the world that lives within us haunts us through visions, dreams and feelings, trying to get our attention. It shows us it's a reality that has possibility and is self-sustaining.

It drives us from the inside, agitating our minds, creating impatience about the outside reality stubbornly holding on and dominating our daily expression as if it were more real, and more valid, more powerful and right than our inner reality.

The two realities compete with each other, each one trying to prove it's greater and more important than the other. We live in an age of multi-tasking, not just in our minute actions and chores but in life itself: multiple careers, families, partners, homes, streams of income. This helps blur our vision even further, leading us to believe living multiple realities is healthy.

So we continue to live two lives. One is our public life, our surface life. It's acceptable, orderly, familiar and safe. It makes some sense, and that keeps us together. It's politically and socially correct. It's based in leadership and authority that tells us this is the way.

The other life, the one that pulls at us from the inside, knows differently. It knows we can be more, do more, matter more.

And oddly, we must deal with these two worlds with the same set of resources. We get no more time or energy to handle our responsibilities as our worlds grow.

One thing that holds us back is our belief that taking responsibility for the planet is a requirement for passage into our vision and purpose. Think how freeing it is to realize it's enough to take responsibility for yourself alone. You can't own purpose. It's too big and requires resources far beyond your scope and know-how. You just need to do your part.

THE SEARCH

Our search for purpose is driven by the pleasure we feel when we get a glimpse of it. We want control over when and how that insight comes to us. This search is also driven by the pain we feel

Living in the demands of 2 realities

DAILY WORLD

- Family, children, work, community, faith
- Citizen responsibility, such as voting, transportation, communication, environment, law
- Technology, including constant interface with the world through computers, telephones, handheld devices, television
- Keeping up with the Joneses, supporting material expectations
- Leadership and politics
- Education
- Survival – putting food on the table
- Safety and security
- Wellness and physical fitness

IDEAL WORLD

- How do I make a difference?
- What is this vision, the quiet force moving ever so slowly in the depth of my core?
- How do I keep my purpose away so I don't have to change?
- How do I bring my purpose into my awareness without it demanding that I hand over my life to it?
- How do I live in the paradox of life's multiple reality?
- How do I respond to the duality in my life that threatens to pull my mind apart?
- What is this undercurrent that pops into my awareness and scrambles my world?
- Why do I get the feeling my life is precariously placed on a shifting, moving, growing foundation that threatens my stability, my sanity and my existence as I know it?
- Why is it that I think I know myself or those close to me, but I know absolutely nothing?
- Will this all fade away at a moment's notice if I don't keep track of it?

when our sense of purpose is absent.

Despite the importance of this quest, it's not practical to pursue your sense of purpose full time every day when you need to survive. You can't sit around and think about purpose when you're trying to figure out how to put food on the table. Purpose is not an interfering force. It emerges when circumstances are appropriate for it, and it judges our life in that moment, coming to us when we have enough energy and the right environment to pay attention to it. This is why your awareness of purpose comes and goes.

I've studied this phenomenon for years as coach and consultant on personal and professional growth and development. My work encourages the individual and the organization to explore what propels us into magnificence and ignites our greatest possible achievement.

People talk to me about purpose, and I've heard their questions evolve over the years. Where once they came out of a philosophical place, rhetorical questions that were full of scholarly curiosity, they now embody an urgency for action and power. People want answers.

- My purpose gives me direction and vision but no power to make it happen.
- My purpose comes to me as passion without an outlet.
- My purpose reveals itself as grandness of vision with no clear way to get there.
- I can't even find my purpose, let alone make it happen.
- I know my purpose is in me. but I can't get my mind wrapped around it enough to make a plan.
- I'm unable to make my purpose logical or practical. It just doesn't make sense to me.
- My desire for purpose creates searching and no solution.
- I hear a voice whispering, calling me to listen, but I can't

seem to translate it into a language I understand.

- I have spent more than $60,000 on this search and I'm still coming up empty.

A great new empowerment has been developing since the 1960s, accelerated by the New Age of the 1980s and the millennial prophecies of the 1990s, followed by the information and communication age and now the virtual age.

I started having intuitions about purpose early in my career. Then a few years ago, it suddenly started to reveal itself in brief flashes. My work is dedicated to developing and embracing human consciousness as it grapples with finding fulfillment of some mysterious drive that pushes us toward our evolution.

The dilemmas we encounter in our inner and outer life circumstances have radically changed since the flower children of the 1960s asked, "Who am I?" and "Why am I here?" Today we ask, "I'm here to do something big, something important, but what is it? I need to get on with whatever it is. Whatever that purpose reveals, I will do it. I'm ready now."

We're living in a purpose-driven time in history. So let's begin to explore how people are experiencing purpose.

There's not a morning I begin without
A thousand questions running through my mind,
That I don't try to find the reason and the logic
In the world that God designed.
The reason why
A bird was given wings,
If not to fly and praise the sky
With every song it sings.
What's right or wrong,
Where I belong
Within the scheme of things...
And why have eyes that see
And arms that reach
Unless you're meant to know
There's something more?
If not to hunger for the meaning of it all,
Then tell me what a soul is for?
Why have the wings
Unless you're meant to fly?
And tell me please, why have a mind
If not to question why?
And tell me where –
Where is it written what it is
I'm meant to be, that I can't dare
To have the chance to pick the fruit of every tree,
Or have my share of every sweet-imagined possibility?

Excerpt from *Where is it Written?*
Sung by Barbara Streisand in *Yentl*
Lyrics by Alan and Marilyn Bergman, Music by Michel Legrand

CHAPTER 2

LOOKING IN THE MIRROR

How do you feel about purpose?

I created a questionnaire about purpose and sent it to 20 people to find out how they feel about this issue. Those people sent it to their friends, relatives and colleagues all over the world, and soon more than 200 responses flooded my e-mail, fax machine and mailbox. Apparently it had hit a hot button.

The people who answered the questionnaire were from different generations, economic backgrounds, family situations and professions. Some showed raw emotion in describing their fear, pain and frustration around the concept of purpose and how to find it. Others expressed excitement and intensity about something they saw as very real but also elusive. Still others tried to explain why they were so disinterested, saying they've never had a sense of purpose and, in some cases, never saw a need for one.

The idea of having a purpose means different things to different people. Take a look at some of the ways people responded. I've grouped their answers under different topics to give you a sense of how the responses varied. First, see for yourself how you answer the questions on the next two pages.

11) What have you achieved along the way that you didn't expect?

_____

12) Are you able to articulate your purpose with anyone else?

_____

13) How have others responded when you've discussed the subject of purpose with them?_____

_____

14) Give examples of other people you know who have found their purpose. Was it helpful to you to hear them describe their experience? _____

_____

15) Do you think there's a formula for finding your purpose?

_____

16) What is the most helpful tool you've found in your search for purpose?_____

_____

17) Are you satisfied with your experience in searching for purpose?

_____

18) What has been your biggest obstacle in this search?_____

_____

19) Have you resolved that obstacle? If so, how?_____

_____

20) What advice would you give someone who is looking for his or her purpose? _____

_____

Purpose Questionnaire

1) Have you ever sensed you have a purpose?_____

_____

2) If so, when do you remember it first starting to come to your attention?_____

_____

3) How did that happen? (In dreams, when you were reading or watching a movie, during a conversation?) _____

_____

4) Do you have any idea what your purpose involves?_____

_____

5) Is it something that was already part of your life or something out of your normal realm?_____

_____

6) How do you think people find their purpose?_____

_____

7) What do you think people are supposed to do with this information once they find it? What is their responsibility toward manifesting their purpose?_____

_____

8) What have you been doing in search of your purpose?_____

_____

9) What have you discovered along the way?_____

_____

10) What have you achieved along the way as planned? _____

_____

HOW OTHERS RESPONDED

The concept of purpose

"Your questionnaire has caused me much reflection, not all of it positive."

"Frankly, the initial response I had to this questionnaire was to ignore it. But something kept telling me to answer it, so I have. Perhaps the reason I have answered this questionnaire is that it gave me an opportunity to express something about my purpose without going into the private details of what that purpose is."

"I found it incredibly moving and worthwhile searching myself to give meaningful answers."

"I think there are many paths to finding one's purpose. People tend to gravitate toward doing something along the lines of purpose because it feels good, centered, grounded, or just right. These experiences happen throughout a lifetime. Perhaps the challenge is in finding the thread that runs through what makes them feel good and making it conscious."

"Manifesting purpose gives meaning and richness to our lives. Finding purpose is the responsibility of the individual, and manifesting the purpose seems to have a place in the grand design. But because we are on different journeys, making a blanket statement about someone else's responsibility to manifest seems to miss the mark."

"Most people say they don't know what their purpose is. I'd say most are afraid to even look for fear their life would be turned upside down."

"I believe everyone and everything has a purpose, which is to awaken to and be one with the universal consciousness, which we all are individualized creations of."

"Defining and recognizing your purpose is an ongoing discipline. It changes according the cycle of one's life. It is part of one's being."

"I have never thought I was born for a purpose or had a particular purpose in life other than being a decent and caring individual. I believe we're just like any other mammal except for the fact we can reason more, ask questions, and seek knowledge about our world and universe. I believe evolution is a fact, and that all life on this planet is evolving, and I'm happy to be along for the ride. I've always thought a lot more about our universe, world, and the life on it than I have ever thought about myself. "

"I believe purpose is very personal and individual to each person, and many find it without knowing anything about the concept."

"A lot of people don't understand it at all. Others think I'm talking about the right job. The last few years, people are testing the waters and now believe that they have invented the meaning of purpose. "

"I must manifest my purpose to be complete. It's what I believe I chose to do 'in spirit' before I came to this world."

"The subject of purpose can be vague to many. However, when discussing the subject with knowledgeable others, it can be a very high energy of 'old souls' coming together in conversation, all adding their own input, experience and education to the discussion. The energy in the room changes, we are all equally evolved, angels gather around for support, and time disappears. ... Those who wear what they think their purpose is can be complete yet incomplete, always focusing on new information, new experiences, anxious to ascend, knowing it is not yet time. I believe there are those who live in and out of other dimensions (more advanced souls) who have more veils lifted and more direct information. "

"As the purpose sheds its light, you slowly start becoming it in a way. I am not so sure you can turn away from it. "

"Once one's purpose is known, it has to engender a passion the person can't ignore. We come in for a reason, and once we know, we have a choice to go forward and manifest our purpose or maybe leave if we choose not to fulfill it in this life."

"I feel a great responsibility for manifesting my own purpose. I think the world could be a better place if people manifested their purpose, as I believe everyone's purpose is both part of your own individual journey as well as part of the master plan of the universe."

"I feel like I'd be letting the rest of the world down if I didn't fulfill my purpose."

"I think some people (lucky ones) know at a very early age exactly what their passion is, and that, in turn, translates into their purpose. I believe there are others who, feeling that something's missing, struggle to find a purpose but are discouraged by the 'burden' of so many choices. And there are those (perhaps also lucky?) who don't seem at all aware of such a thing as purpose, but simply go along on a superficial path without delving into matters of the soul: Who am I? Why am I here? What am I destined to do?"

"Who has found their purpose and is living it? Oprah. She's an example of finding our purpose and growing within it. She's somewhat unchanged in many ways, even though her purpose has spiritually fulfilled and changed her. Once you've found your purpose, growing within it is not necessarily as important as living it."

Searching for purpose

"I have always had a feeling or sense of purpose in my life. My search for purpose has been my only driving force and focus. Even as a child, I knew very deeply that I was born for some purpose or to do something that could make a significant impact on humanity."

"When I look back at the experience of seeking my purpose, I accomplished a lot. I was very curious, which took me down a lot of roads. It was like I was blindly walking and not knowing what I was doing. I sometimes think it could have been easier, but then it was what it was. Sometimes I think I just wasted a lot of time. I don't know for sure if I succeeded, but what I do know is that I don't have this driving force toward it anymore. At some point, I just gave up."

"I seemed to focus on everyday matters and kept the purpose in the background. I did not search for it. It found me. I feel it has added an extra dimension to my life and a depth to how I am in this world."

"I do have some innate sense of what my purpose may involve, but it is not clear."

"Sometimes I get glimpses of purpose in conversation and reading. It's a feeling that things are coming together."

"I don't feel I search for purpose. I recognize I have it or it exists."

"My purpose has always been a part of my life as I realize it today; however, I did do considerable research through readings, seminars, books, etc., to reach that conclusion…. I have followed many exercises given me from readings, books, meditation, affirmations, videos… following the advice of others. Now I just live my purpose every day, knowing it's as simple as just being who I am."

"Most of the difficult things in my life have moved me to the next part, and now I'm pretty comfortable with being uncomfortable at times, because I'm sure the next thing is supposed to happen."

"I was starting to have so many visions, insights, moments of deja vu and remembered dreams, I was afraid I'd lose track of them all if I didn't record them. At the time, I was busy with small children and my life was too difficult to do anything about these fantasies of becoming an artist – fantasies that made me feel so good. As the years passed, my artistic purpose became clearer as I met other artists who were actually doing what I was only fantasizing: playing with paint and other materials."

"In my personal journey, I came to understand that I am the Purpose. It's a state of being. It is not something I have to do or that is outside myself. I always sensed I had a purpose and I spent many years looking for it … until I realized I have to do nothing except be myself."

"As soon as I can just be exactly who I was meant to be, I will then be able to fulfill my highest purpose."

"My feeling is I should just move toward what feels best and what interests me. I think that's how we find our way, although I can't say I know what my purpose is. Along the path so far, I have experienced many highs and lows, had a career, a family, tried lots of adventurous things, traveled a lot, and had some bad times, too. I don't know if I will ever know I've found my purpose because I don't think I have completed what I'm supposed to do yet. Perhaps it changes as we take the steps to evolve and grow. Perhaps it's just learning to enjoy the simple things along the way of life, maybe to finally realize that we are the creator and God is us. I can't say I know many people who believe they have found their purpose. Or, if they feel this is 'it' right now, it seems to change with life as we get older."

"I still don't understand my purpose. I know it has something to do with relationship, but it doesn't bother me not to know what it is. My purpose is my life."

"I carefully choose those people I discuss the subject of purpose with, and most of them are like-minded, so they believe in the concept. I think there are some who are afraid of the idea of purpose and the implications it may have on their lives."

"I try to surround myself with people who have pieces of the puzzle I'm trying to put together. This is a large and growing collection. Some of them know about purpose and passion. Others know about how to communicate what they're thinking and feeling. Others know how to ask people about their own sense of purpose. Through these fascinating people, I learn every day."

"I'm excited about purpose, and about digging deeper. It didn't throw me into a state of fear, not at all."

"It really is amazing. I think there are a lot of people out there who don't think about it, and they'll go to their graves not even wondering about a purpose, and that's OK, too. And that's where I think the awareness comes in. An awareness, or a spiritual seeking, and I think people who are looking for a purpose and don't know what it is, my suggestion is that they could start volunteering."

Frustration

"I am mostly satisfied with the information that comes to me. Sometimes, however, I feel impatient for more and faster information, but as I am always busy and find life so entertaining, I soon forget the impatience. And before long, new information arrives and surprises me."

"I am not going to talk about purpose too much because I am so disheartened and viewing things from such an egotistical point view. I'm so frustrated as a human being, the whole notion of purpose pushes my buttons."

"My purpose has never been clear. It has never been even kind of, sort of a little bit clear. This makes me angry and resentful, and I feel cheated. Being attentive and attuned to discovering my purpose has caused me endless frustration and futility. I started being drawn to metaphysical questions about 20 years ago, and I feel no closer now to any sense of clarity about purpose than I did then."

"I remember first wondering about purpose in the third grade. That was my second year in grade school as I 'skipped' first grade after about six weeks. I remember wondering about the purpose of insects. ...I have wondered if life has a purpose in general, and, in particular whether I have a purpose. I have pondered whether the purpose of man is similar or different to the purpose of ants. I have not, as of this date, resolved any of this and do not know whether I have a purpose or even whether it is a reasonable question to ask."

"I am satisfied and sometimes frustrated."

"I have never felt a sense of purpose in my life. Maybe it's something I am missing, or that I should be seeking, but when I look at others desperately seeking purpose but letting life and the ability to do others good go by because they are seeking something 'higher,' then I really struggle with it. I do whatever I can for people, sometimes when they ask, sometimes I get the opportunity to do so before they need to ask, but I do not see that as a sense of purpose, more a sense of doing what is right."

"Truthfully, I don't know if I have a purpose."

"I thought purpose would involve my efforts on a much grander scale."

"I was in my early 30s is when my sense of purpose hit pretty strongly. All of a sudden, I realized going through life feeling numb to the experience was not a good thing, and I felt a growing connection to 'something more.' Now I know what it is, but I sure as $@# don't know how to manifest it. That is my opportunity at this juncture in my journey."

"I have never felt a strong drive in any direction. My life has been spent just making ends meet. I envy people who have found their destiny."

"Just drifting is not a positive option anymore for me. ... The inner frustration has been the hardest thing to deal with, the constant picking yourself up and dusting yourself off and starting all over again."

"I have not discussed my Purpose in life as I see it with anyone else. It is my own private matter."

"Have I ever sensed I had a purpose? Yes, because I wanted to. Do I have one? I don't know."

"Is my fear nothing but a stumbling block to what's beyond?"

"I have had no experience of anything. I fulfill my obligations – sometimes it's fun, OK, and sometimes it's not. My world is small and I just try to be present with what is. ... My commitments and responsibilities, I meet. Obviously this isn't working or I would be driven to or be something/ where/one else. I probably help the people who I have contact with knowingly or unknowingly, and maybe that's all there is. ... I didn't expect I would be on this path so long and still have no inkling. ... It has been very frustrating and painful now for years, not fun, not an adventure. I give up. No surrender, just resigned. I feel I'm just not getting it. Nothing in my life lights me up, and I negate the possibility now."

Discovery

"I've found that one thing has always led to the next, to the next, to the next, and I have added my experiences together to get closer and closer to fulfilling my purpose."

"It seems the universe and human life within it must be purposeful. Otherwise, what's the point of incarnating and reincarnating? As long as I can remember, I've felt there was a grand overarching design to life, but couldn't quite grab a hold of it! Just sensing there was a 'story' or blueprint somewhere and wondering how to find it ... it is clear to me I have a purpose that is being revealed to me step by step."

"My sense of purpose evolved over time. I was depressed and could not imagine why on earth I was here. I kept asking the question, 'Is this it?'

"In discovering my purpose, I first had to begin to discover my authentic self, who I really was and what I meant to be. My purpose includes the essence of who I am."

"I have, and am, learning a lot of hard lessons and adjustments, and am humbled and awestruck by the "big picture" that is starting to be revealed to me, and understanding that every human being can choose to be part of an evolving universe and changing consciousness. I'm very grateful to be part of all this, and for the attendant excitement and expansion of my life."

"Discovering purpose was a very slow and gradual process. I can't remember any big aha moments. … When I look back at my life's activities, interests and education, I realize purpose was an unconscious part of me all along the way."

"Fear became my guide. I promised myself I would do whatever scared me. I gradually move further into purpose. …Where my excitement and aliveness and fear are great in combination with discovery and expression, that's where I find myself. …I feel like I'm getting feedback from the universe that I'm moving in the right direction."

"Discovering my sense of purpose was never a happening. It was an awareness as long as I can remember. I am inner-directed, so it was natural for me to retreat to the woods outside our home and spend many hours just reflecting and learning. With this awareness, you have a love for others that does not judge them, just shares with them when asked and supports them to know all that they are as it is appropriate."

"I'm happy with what I've discovered this far. However, I don't think I'll be satisfied until I'm leaving this world. Then I'll know I've completed what I was here to do. I'm not good at waiting, so I guess I wish I had a better handle on exactly what it is that I'm here for now."

"It does kind of give you chills when you look at the big picture. I was recently on a road trip with a friend of mine, and she said, "I wonder what my purpose is. I said, 'You know, you've raised children, you're now taking care of your mother. I think maybe that's your purpose.' We're not all called to greatness."

"I knew then clear as a bell that the most important thing I would ever do would be to have kids. Ironically, I have always had to fight for what I've always known, and that has been the hardest part of knowing. And then having kids was not that easy for me. For me, knowing my purpose was the easy part! And if you're laughing at me because I have totally missed my purpose in life, well then hurry up with that book, because I'll really need it."

Acceptance

"I have this driving force in my life that demands I keep to my purpose. … No matter how I may try to 'get out of it,' no matter how I may beg and pray to be relieved of the duty, in the end any 'satisfaction' involves the deep knowledge that I simply must do what I am destined to do, and I will die knowing I gave it my best shot."

"I only know my sense of purpose became a deep knowledge within me – somewhat like a vision. In 1991, I had a second vision that, as I look at it now, was an 'adjunct' to the first purpose and a real help in keeping faith in my purpose."

"At this moment, I don't feel I have free will when it comes to my purpose. I just do it, and when I'm done, I'll leave the planet."

"Having a purpose gives you a reason to live – a reason to get up in the morning. It helps a lot to make your journey fun and it makes you a happy and energetic person. I feel very lucky to have a purpose."

"Living with purpose was out of my consciousness…my value was in what I did, not in who I am."

"I was born with one big purpose, and everything else is an insight but does not change the purpose."

"Purpose is beyond my daily consideration and concern. Rather than purpose, I look to service. Daily life is not a function of purpose, its focus is on healing and serving. That is how I can relate to purpose on a daily basis."

"Jesus said He is the way, the truth, and the life. I know for sure He has a purpose for those who seek Him and that purpose has not even been in your wildest dreams. Seek Him and He will take you where you have never dreamed of."

"I feel guided and alone. It's as if I am being guided to understand what I need to do in any given moment but am all alone to do it. Although how I express my desire/ultimate goal has changed, my commitment has not faltered. In the toughest of times, I always come back to my commitment, and this commitment is preparing me for my ultimate goal."

"My natural purpose is to always come from my heart in all I do and be an appropriate example for all I meet. I believe I have a bigger purpose and more significant purpose by helping create a foundation which will assist in creating heaven on Earth. Ideas and intentions seem to change for me as I change."

"Following this purpose is key to fulfillment and happiness. The responsibility is to yourself to pursue the highest level you can with your purpose. There is also a duty to the universe (mankind) for each person to pursue purpose as it ties into a purpose for the greater whole."

"I started out thinking my purpose was to serve humanity, and then it was to embody my soul, and then it was to…it keeps changing. As I progress, I keep focusing on what I think my current purpose is, and then, wham! It's different."

"My purpose is who I am, not something outside myself. I think that's everybody's purpose. We are here to express who we are. We are light, we are love, we are joy. It's not something you have to do, or to help, to feel joy. That's who we are. It's not something in your mind, it's your whole being. You have to have hope in your heart. When I go to my heart, there is no room for pain, only love."

"I do sense I have a purpose. I think I have always felt it, even when I was young. It was basically just a knowing. It's not clear to me what my purpose is. I feel it's in another realm now, although that may change."

"Mother Teresa said something that really had an impact on me a couple of years ago: If you do small things with great love, bingo! There's your purpose. So to me, every day is a purpose. I might not always be kind, or charitable, or whatever, but every day I get up, to me, is now a purpose of doing something good for someone. Some kind of compassion or empathy or something. It makes my day go a lot better."

Obstacles

"I'm afraid I haven't sensed my purpose, and after spending years being driven to trying to find it, I have kind of given up. There's no struggle, nor is there any fulfillment. I have no sense of what I'm doing here on this earth. I'm just here, and although I can't say I really accept being here for no reason, I certainly do not have any inkling of why."

"My biggest inner obstacle has been fear: fear of facing myself, fear of disappointment, fear of failing."

"Emotions have been more of an inhibiting factor than I expected."

"My biggest obstacle has been dealing with minutiae, the everyday matters that tend to take away my concentration about the bigger picture."

"My biggest obstacle is a combo of my perception that I don't have enough time to search and then I don't trust myself enough. I have not completely resolved this as of yet."

"I would have appreciated a teacher. It has been real hard sometimes, and lonely."

"I don't understand hate for someone who has never harmed you. I don't understand using someone just because you can. I don't understand judgment of others because they're not like you. Variety is what makes this world so interesting and exciting. Politics, religion – why can't people allow others to make their own decisions to follow the beliefs that bring them happiness? If it doesn't hurt others, then why do people make it their business to ridicule a different approach to things? Another obstacle would be false authority, people preying on others who are searching for their truth or purpose, taking money in excess instead of merely helping. People not admitting to not knowing."

"Each obstacle has become a steppingstone to understanding…and thus one step closer to completion."

"The biggest obstacles are issues related to day-to-day living, such as earning money, family responsibilities, job duties. It's easy to put your purpose on a back burner and take the much easier path of doing nothing."

"I have not done much, and that makes me anxious, somewhat guilty and somewhat sad that I've not used the gifts I have. A very strong sense of guilt – that I have not explored my purpose enough, that having my life is such a gift I must give back, I must, but I don't know how or what or to whom."

"Purpose is part of my life because my Creator is part of my life. God created me for a purpose, so I would say yes, it has always been part of my life. The biggest obstacle is constantly thinking I know what is best vs. God knowing. Prayer and scripture reading is how it is resolved, but it is ongoing."

"Starting my life from a blue-collar survival place, I wasn't exposed to the leadership and coaching I needed until later in life. I have turned a corner in the past few years, and I now have a lot of valuable coaching in my life."

"There are constant things that distract you from even being aware of the possibility of purpose, much less actually finding it."

"The biggest obstacle is just imagining what my purpose might be. I don't think I've ever searched for purpose. Just worked hard at paying bills, keeping from getting my material goods repossessed. I know that sounds sad, but I guess most of my life I've just struggled to keep my head above water."

Advice

"Teachings are what the intellect understands and are often very helpful, but wisdom is what the heart and soul know, because they have lived it. Maybe, after all, we learn our purpose only by living it out."

"Be curious about yourself and your place in the world. Be curious about how you operate, what you find enjoyable and problematic. Use your body to help validate your steps. Be assured each of us has an important role to play in healing the universe ... and no one is better than another."

"Ponder those things that open your heart and make your soul sing. And for those of us who have a rather stubborn nature, take heart in this wise old saying: 'Today's mighty oak is just yesterday's nut that held its ground.' As a gal who was born 30 years too soon and who was always bordering on heresy in my life in the Christian church, and lived long enough to see how others came around to thinking in a different way, too, it still gives me hope for the future!"

"Search for ways to live your life so you will do some good. The answer will come."

"Just do what makes you happy and don't worry about it. It happens."

"Meditate in whatever form. Tuning in makes sense to the individual. Follow your nose, be very mindful, and constantly review where you're going, where you've been, and constantly try and refine yourself and every aspect of your life."

"If you're lucky enough to find guidance, value and honor it for the incredible gift it is. Never take anything for granted. Retain a beginner's mind, be awestruck, and try always to be in touch with your passion and ecstasy."

"Unfortunately, there is no formula – except listening and acting on it. Trust. Allow yourself to be true to the moment."

"There must be a reason for being here. Pay attention to coincidences and explore them. I would if these things were in my conscious awareness."

"Keep your heart open, and pack a lot of patience. Create a happy and satisfying life for yourself outside of the question of purpose, so if it never shows up, you still have something to show for having been alive."

"If you keep working at it and never waver, it will manifest at just the right time. "

"I think being grateful and appreciating each and every thing and being that comes into your life to help you get closer to your purpose speeds up the entire process. When prayers of any kind are answered or even said, saying thank you afterward helps with the manifestation and the guides want to assist you as much as they can."

"Stop trying so hard. Believe the time and place are as important as the purpose itself. Honor and respect the fact that when things aren't ready, things aren't ready. Have the patience a greater power than you knows when the best time is."

"The potential grandness of my contribution keeps me going. In order to feel positive feelings, you need to endure the negative ones as well. Acknowledge the polarity. Open your heart, and you cannot be in fear."

"Find yourself and be true to who you find."

"The fun is in the journey."

"My first suggestion would be to recognize our God-given gifts and talents. Second, I would ask, 'What are you passionate about?' or 'What makes your heart hurt?' and go from there."

"I suppose if someone wanted to know his or her purpose, there could be many ways and paths. …However, it is just possible that purpose finds you when you're ready."

"Purpose just evolves, but I know one thing: It will happen gently and not with any kind of 'slap in the head.' It will just get embodied, and then all of a sudden it will just be."

REFLECTING ON WHAT YOU NEED TO KNOW

When we look in the mirror, we always want to see something other than what we are. At the same time, we're always hoping we are what we see. This is a human trait.

The reason we are seeking purpose is to find the satisfaction that comes from the act of searching. Do we ever really know our purpose, fully and definitively? As one survey respondent said:

Accept that you don't need to know everything, but trust you will know what you need to know. Searching might not work, because it might be only your ego's need for security. Your purpose will reveal itself when you are ready to respond. The butterfly might land in your open hands.

YOU WON'T SUCCEED BY FOLLOWING SOMEONE ELSE'S PATH. SO YOU'D BETTER SPEND SOME TIME FOCUSING ON YOUR OWN PATH AND YOUR OWN PURPOSE.

– DONALD TRUMP

IF NO ONE EVER TEACHES YOU TO DREAM THE UNLIMITED DREAM, IF NO ONE EVER TEACHES YOU TO BREATHE THE BREATH OF THE UNIVERSE IN SPRING, AND IF NO ONE EVER TEACHES YOU TO LOOK AT THE MIDNIGHT SKY AND CONTEMPLATE THE CONCEPTS OF FOREVER, IF NO ONE EVER TEACHES YOU THIS, THEN YOU WILL BE FOREVER SEPARATED FROM YOUR GREATEST BEING.

– RAMTHA

CHERISH YOUR VISIONS. CHERISH YOUR IDEALS. CHERISH THE MUSIC THAT STIRS IN YOUR HEART, THE BEAUTY THAT FORMS IN YOUR MIND, THE LOVELINESS THAT DRAPES YOUR PUREST THOUGHTS, FOR OUT OF THEM WILL GROW ALL DELIGHTFUL CONDITIONS, ALL HEAVENLY ENVIRONMENT; OF THESE, IF YOU BUT REMAIN TRUE TO THEM, YOUR WORLD WILL AT LAST BE BUILT.

– JAMES ALLEN

DESPERATELY SEEKING PURPOSE

CHAPTER 3

A DRIVING FORCE

Do you have a sense of your purpose?

Some people are born with a very concise individual purpose. It seems to be programmed into their DNA, as if they contain a seed that's destined to grow into a defined individual expression. It pushes them, shoves them, becomes a priority in their lives. It comes out of a place within them, it feels big, and they know it's important, even giant.

Others have a feeling they were born to be a part of something bigger than their individual expression in life. They sense each person is a piece of the magnificent expression of human potential. This subconscious knowledge runs quietly under the surface of daily awareness. They don't know what to do about it. They don't know what it is, but they get it in bits and pieces. They can't really talk about it because expressing anything about it feels too personal. But when they hear other people talk about it, they slowly realize their purpose is only a small piece of a much bigger, global expression.

Then there are people who don't seem to have any programming about purpose whatsoever. They can't consciously reference any sense of purpose. Some of them find this frustrating while others shrug it off as unimportant.

Whether you feel a sense of purpose or not, a global movement is affecting your life. You're surrounded by signs of it everywhere you turn. Popular books, television shows, films, Internet sites and music all seek answers to our purpose here on earth. You see and hear the questions in political debates, environmental discussions, advertisements, news stories and conversations that can occur almost anywhere.

Yet, when exploring purpose, many people can't get past the question of their personal part in it, or their individual mission.

The sense of purpose comes with vision, knowing, intuition, all kinds of things, but it's seldom clear. There's an extremely strong sense that this purpose will give them the deep fulfillment that's missing in their lives.

Some people say this sense of purpose can make them want to give up everything else in life because it feels so important. The urging and desire for purpose can be so powerful, they question whether it's real or they're just making it up.

My dedication to this subject comes out of the emotional chaos it evokes in so many. The spectrum of feelings is astounding, from the most negative, agitated and aggressive, to introspective, pensive and resigned, to curious, excited and exhilarated, and everything in between.

I created a list of the feelings expressed in interviews and responses to the Desperately Seeking Purpose Questionnaire, and it was more than six pages long. The descriptive words took into account more feelings than I thought possible on a single subject. On the next several pages, you'll find excerpts from some of the answers about people's feelings on purpose.

Feelings about purpose

- It's an unknown obligation.
- I'm not good enough, not smart enough, not whatever enough.
- The longing to discover it overshadows my life.
- I'm too scared to think about it, let alone search.
- I've given up on finding it.
- I have a burning desire to find it.
- It causes tremendous self-doubt.
- What if I don't do it right?
- Some searching for purpose has been hijacked by religion.
- It stimulates the desire to be greater than the mundane.
- I feel empowered to stretch beyond what I thought were my limits.
- I'm saddened by the subject.
- I'm ashamed and disappointed in myself and life.
- I'm disheartened.
- I judge myself by other people's standards.
- I feel satisfied and fulfilled.
- I don't believe I have a purpose.
- It's not fun, it's painful and a struggle, so I'm resigned to not having a purpose.
- I am never clear, which makes me feel angry, resentful and cheated.
- The subject causes me endless frustration.
- It's an exercise in futility.
- People find purpose through grace.
- I'm not worthy or qualified.
- I don't fit in because I don't know my purpose.
- It's my inner driving force.

- I feel like I've wasted my time looking for it.
- I have this fear of failing myself and others.
- Others judge me with disbelief.
- No one is on the same page.
- I'm guarded about sharing my feelings on this.
- It's my own private business.
- Sometimes I'm clear on it, and sometimes dark and foggy.
- It brings me bliss, joy and freedom.
- Emotions inhibit my search.
- Fantasies make my life a roller coaster.
- Real life keeps getting in the way.
- My sense of purpose energizes me.
- Dealing with minutiae interrupts my search.
- Having a sense of purpose is threatening to others.
- It takes more time than I have.
- I don't trust myself to know my purpose when I find it.
- The search leaves me questioning and alone.
- Dealing with purpose takes too much commitment, obligation and responsibility.
- It makes me crazy, making everyone else crazy.
- It makes me furious.
- It's easy to get derailed, off track and discouraged.
- The search is challenging physically, mentally and emotionally.
- I have no clue how to find my purpose.
- Thinking about it leads me to disappointment and judgment of others.
- People think I'm crazy, and most of the time I know I'm not.
- I must be wrong if no one else can understand me.

- I don't know, but I do know it's a terrible paradox.
- It is my core belief.
- It's a moral end point.
- It brings a deep satisfaction and healing that give me peace of mind.
- I feel disconnected and skeptical.
- Hopefully I will come to know self-love and true self-worth.
- I feel liberated.
- I am grateful.
- I found myself, even though I never really thought I was lost.
- I have a new consciousness.
- Purpose is a burden.
- Only lucky people have purpose.
- Believing in purpose takes a leap of faith.
- To thine own self be true.
- I crave more of everything good and joyful.
- I feel a peaceful existence and confidence in myself.
- I'm not as good as others in spirit.
- I'm leading from my heart.
- I feel a lightheartedness.
- I'm afraid of the consequences.
- I feel this irrational drive to search for purpose.
- My searches have come up empty.
- It requires acceptance and compliance.
- I have an innate sense of purpose, but not clear answers.
- Guilt and shame get in my way.
- It's the key to fulfillment and happiness.
- It takes a lot of self-reflection.

The passion of these responses, and the emotional struggle they represent, prompted me to write this book at this time. Along with the "bigness" of the purpose they embody, there seems to be an equally united sense of urgency. Those who sense they have a purpose are being called into action, some for the first time. They don't want to miss the chance to do or be what they came into this life to fulfill.

THE SENSE OF PURPOSE

When I look more closely at the whole phenomenon of needing, wanting, having and acting on the passions that drive us toward our purpose, it seems it's not as important for people to *know their purpose* as it is to *have a sense that it exists.*

In the questionnaire, I asked, "Do you have a sense of your purpose?" As long as people have this feeling, they move forward. Losing the sense of purpose is depressing, even if you still don't know what the purpose involves.

In fact, when asked "Do you have a sense that you have a purpose?" the response is overwhelmingly "yes." But when asked "Do you know what your purpose is and what your responsibility is toward manifesting that purpose?" people experience confusion and extreme frustration. It's in this space between having a sense of purpose and actually having a defined purpose where the desperate search and self-doubt set in.

What is it about this subject that drives us? It's hope. It's like a river that flows within us, and things we do can draw from it. But there's no exact formula for how to define purpose or how to get it. That's what makes it so special. When we do align with it, we feel a shock wave through our whole being. Our mind, body, spirit and emotions remember this feeling like it's burned into us forever.

The moment of profound ecstasy that comes from connecting with that purpose resonates inside us. No other goal or achievement is as extraordinary as one that has touched into life purpose.

Following that sense of purpose can become an obsession, like chasing a high. It can become addictive and make you feel heady. You do anything to connect with it again, throwing yourself into one effort after another.

And if you lose focus and turn away from it for a moment, your sense of purpose can disappear, sending you crashing down as the feeling fades away. The periods of exhilaration – those exquisite, heart-opening, soul-moving, spirit-filled moments – then vanish without a trace, leaving no clues about how they can be reproduced.

GOALS AND ACHIEVEMENTS

This time in the world is marked by extraordinary economic achievement. More than ever before, people are reaching for the stars. They're becoming rich through real estate investments, technological advances, global collaboration over the Internet, and even contests on reality TV shows.

Our ability to achieve has increased substantially – but not our purpose. That has stayed the same.

People are looking at this new world of magnificent achievement and calling it purpose. People who feel they can't reach the heights of achievement they see around them become convinced they're not among the privileged who were born with a purpose, so they throw away their chance at communion with this elusive experience. They feel inadequate, resentful, jealous and frustrated.

I gnore what anyone else tells you about your purpose. Regardless of what anyone might say to you, the truth about your feeling purposeful is that only you can know it, and if you don't feel it in that inner place where a burning desire resides, it isn't your purpose. Your relatives and friends may attempt to convince you that what they feel is your destiny. They may see talents that they think will help you make a great living, or they may want you to follow in their footsteps because they think you'll be happy doing what they've done for a lifetime. Your skill at mathematics or decorating or fixing electronic equipment might indicate a high aptitude for a given pursuit – but in the end, if you don't feel it, nothing can make it resonate with you.

– *Wayne Dyer*

The sense of purpose directs us toward the what but not the how. So we do what we know how to do and hope it will lead us or turn into what we know in our deepest being – hence the overachievement, the mistakes, the start-ups and start-overs, the wrong turns, the unfulfilled, the unfinished, the big dreams that go bust or don't get off the ground, the false starts and the lack of clarity that prevent starts. In the face of these obstacles, our intention, goodwill, passion and conviction can run dry.

But here's some good news: We live our purpose no matter what.

The key is to be able to recognize our purpose and connect with it so we can get pleasure from living it. So the sense of purpose is the bridge, holding us in that hope and possibility. The sense of purpose keeps us going.

Finding and shaping your life purpose is the most important thing you'll ever do. The sense of purpose is the driving force that spawns all the achievements you will ever accomplish. It provides an unlimited source of motivation that drives you to achieve all the goals you set for yourself and enables you to live life to the fullest.

Your purpose is inextricably linked to your dreams. Your sense of purpose is the force that propels you forward, enabling you to wake up every morning and engage in meaningful work. The drive for purpose can become a powerful and positive motivation behind everything you do.

Your relationship with your sense of purpose

- The sense of purpose reveals your true self and requires you to embrace your personal truth.

- This purpose is unmistakable, and its existence is crystal-clear. When you first start to talk about it, any attempt to verbalize it seems to backfire, and you feel like the fool once again.

- Dreams, passions and visions can bring you closer to connecting with deeper places inside yourself where your purpose might reside.

- The sense of purpose emits moments of exhilaration. It's not all hard work and seriousness.

- Goals, actions and achievements might or might not leave your sense of purpose fulfilled.

- You can't will your purpose to be anything other than what it is.

- The sense of purpose can evoke conviction, courage and joy, as well as exasperation, anger and self-doubt.

- We intersect with our sense of purpose while we go through everyday life.

- You will give up the search only to try it again in a different way with a different perspective, attitude and intention.

MISCONCEPTIONS

People confuse purpose with goals, intention and passion. Purpose might be something you really love, or it might not. Purpose is bigger. Goals are the steps you take to get to purpose. Intention keeps your mind and emotions on track. Goals, achievements, service, helping others or doing something you love are ways to interface with purpose, but those are not purpose.

Many believe life purpose is about doing something. We're convinced we add the most meaning to our lives through our actions. As a result, we regularly face painful questions such as:

Am I doing the right thing?

Am I doing enough?

Am I doing it well enough?

What if I'm putting all this effort into doing something that is not my real purpose?

What if I do all this and still feel unfulfilled?

Life purpose is not the doing, it is the being. Living life purpose is not about doing or doing enough. Doing is significant, and it has a place in our lives, but it's wise to put doing in second place to being. Life purpose involves being aligned with your truth and knowing your inner power.

Life purpose can mean ultimate fulfillment, which has nothing to do with doing. Fulfillment comes through the experience of expressing your true self in your daily life first and sometimes in the world.

Fulfillment, love, compassion, frustration, and even fear can be stimulated in your search for purpose but are not necessarily related to purpose. It's not even the creative force that vibrates in every cell of your body and expands your imagination, forcing extraordinary visions of possibility to fill your head. All these things and more are not purpose. They are the symptoms that purpose exists.

When people reduce their purpose to a goal, they lose it. It becomes something to be achieved, and the expansiveness and brilliance of it disappears into a task, a job or work.

If you focus on doing, you'll miss the point. You'll miss out on the adventure of unfolding who you are in the world. You'll risk putting time and effort into paths that don't reflect who you are, paths that lead to a life that's empty and unfulfilling. Doing things that don't reflect who you are is a waste of life force.

Purpose is global, not restricted or limited by geographic boundaries, education, culture, religion, race, nationality or socioeconomic status. It's also not personal, even though it feels like something secret inside. It's an entirely global collaboration. It belongs to the planet. It does not require action or prerequisites to be fulfilled or completed.

The small number of us who do have the vision of purpose are in a very fortunate position. We're here to make a difference.

The tragedy is that so many of the most highly evolved people on the planet are still lost in an emotional and psychological relationship to life that's very basic and keeps their manifestation of purpose limited. However, the time is coming, and an urgency and excitement are pushing the evolution into the forefront of our minds. The ability to fulfill purpose doesn't really have to do with a particular individual. Because of the enormity of the task, the only thing that makes a difference is how much people actually want to live their purpose.

Others around you might or might not understand your pursuit, but you will know with certainty why you continue to seek purpose. The act of seeking it has intrinsic value that you will conclude is more important than anything else imaginable.

41

Symptoms of the seed of global purpose

- The feelings and thoughts provoked by the sense of purpose are often irrational, illogical and, at times, seemingly insane, but the drive remains to discover it.

- Purpose comes with the passion of knowing that overshadows any attempts internally or externally to deny it or shut it down.

- Purpose is dormant in the unconscious most of the time. It awakens and reveals itself just enough to make you crazy, and then disappears.

- Determining how to manifest your purpose can be so overwhelming that you become numb to it and attempt repeatedly to turn away from it.

- Your exact purpose is almost impossible to identify in real-life terms and descriptions sometimes, but you keep trying. You can't give up. It's the thing of most value in your life.

- Your true purpose can't be denied, faked or imitated. There are no knock-offs, and it can't be disguised or effectively be channeled into short-term goals and achievements.

- Insight about purpose might come to you when you least expect it – during a crisis, during a celebration, very late in life or during times of quiet or while you're researching something else.

LIVING YOUR PURPOSE

True happiness doesn't come from riches, fast cars, big houses or perfect partners. It comes from living your purpose.

Finding your purpose might be a lifelong pursuit or you might have discovered it when you were 5 years old. There's no absolute timeline for anyone. That's a good reason never to give up, to keep on discovering things every day. It's also a terrific recipe for a successful life. Following your own path will bring you to the places you were meant to be. Expand your horizons! In other words, think big and live large.

You don't have to set aside additional time to live your purpose. You live it while in motion.

You can live your purpose while doing what you're doing right now, or you can look for new ways of expressing it. Expressing your purpose through soulful living is like putting your life on an emotional and mental diet: You find yourself naturally moving toward activities that allow you to express your personal truth and you will live your life more fully and in alignment with the power within you. You'll find that your life will become much less complicated and emotionally charged.

Your life purpose is a lifelong journey or commitment without any discernable stopping point. The reason for this is that if you set life purpose with an achievable end point, such as saying Thomas Edison's life purpose was inventing the light bulb, then what do you do with your life after your purpose is completed? Anthony Robbins in his audio book *Live With Passion* states that many adult males die within a few years of retiring, not of old age or of poor health, but simply because they no longer have anything purposeful to live for.

From The Purpose of Life is to Live a Life of Purpose
by Adam Eisenstat, Trump University website

DISCOVERIES ON THE WAY

Purpose is like a path we follow during our long journey through life. Your sense of purpose is, by its very nature, something that captures your passion.

Your purpose is between your innermost wisdom and your ultimate power. The closer you get to what that looks, acts and feels like, the more you'll know you're being purposefully guided and aligned. You will feel mysteriously drawn from the inside to living your purpose.

In the survey, I asked people what they discovered in their quest for purpose that they didn't expect. They wrote personal

---

What people discovered while searching for purpose

- Delighted and amazed at what life really can be, and I have an important part in it.

- Purpose found me and I live it every day.

- It adds an extra dimension to my life.

- It sparks in me a feeling of infinite possibilities, drawing me deep into discovery of myself.

- It's a process in a flow that takes time and patience I seldom have.

- Purpose is me. It's who I am.

- It reminds me of the importance of my commitment, my responsibility to myself and to mankind, what my life is really about.

- I recovered my true self.

- I've learned to speak up for my truth. I now know my input matters and is important, and that I actively contribute to the awakening of consciousness.

- Purpose is a lifestyle. It's become the way I live my life, and it guides the choices I make.

---

discovery, true self, self-responsibility and personal power.

Living purpose is a lifelong quest, not a day-by-day thing. It's a long-distance trek rather than a sprint to a goal and then the question "What's next?"

That means if you miss a day in your search for purpose, it doesn't matter, as long as you enjoy the journey.

THERE ARE NO EXTRA PIECES IN THE UNIVERSE. EVERYONE IS HERE BECAUSE HE OR SHE HAS A PLACE TO FILL, AND EVERY PIECE MUST FIT ITSELF INTO THE BIG JIGSAW PUZZLE.

– DEEPAK CHOPRA

CONSCIOUSNESS CAN ONLY EVOLVE THROUGH ME, AND IT WON'T HAPPEN UNLESS I WHOLEHEARTEDLY AND UNCONDITIONALLY GIVE MYSELF TO THAT PROCESS.

– ANDREW COHEN

ACCEPT WHO YOU ARE AND REVEL IN THAT.

– MITCH ALBOM

CHAPTER 4

WE'RE IN THIS TOGETHER

How are we responsible for manifesting our purpose?
Everyone has a part in manifesting our global purpose, both individually and collectively, consciously and unconsciously. We are all participating in this dance of human expansion. Each piece is as important as any other.

In order to make sense of this massive growth that has engaged humanity, it's helpful to have access to a bigger picture of what's going on. The plans for this project lie within each individual, but no one person or group holds the whole burden of responsibility. We're in this together. We actually are working in teams.

Each generation hold clues to how we as a species are supposed to develop and implement this monumental project of purpose. The evolution of the consciousness takes more than the vigilant participation of a single village. It takes the entire planet.

The different generations are classified according to key characteristics. These groupings are not arbitrary. There's a continuum between the generations, with changes in attitude slowly shifting as each group, through its actions and attitudes, encourages the world to change.

People who live in a certain time in history and human development share more than just music, fads, inventions and knowledge of the day's pop culture. They're also united in the way their generation shapes the values, ethics and attitudes about the world.

Of course, not everyone in each generation fits perfectly within the description of that group or exhibits all of its characteristics. But you can use the categories and generalizations as a guide to understand each team and who is doing what, and this gives you more clarity about yourself and your individual contribution. This knowledge helps empower you to take ownership of your part in this global human endeavor.

THE LAST 5 GENERATIONS

Before we look at the role of each generation in supporting greater purpose, which we will do later in this chapter, let's first examine how the generations are commonly defined. Each is known for distinct characteristics, work styles, consumer habits, spiritual and religious beliefs, and popular culture preferences. This gives us an idea of how different the generations are.

Silent Generation (approximately 1930 to 1945)

This group was raised to believe commitment, responsibility and conformity are tickets to success. Sometimes referred to as traditionalists, or as suffocated children of the Great Depression, they learned children are to be seen and not heard. On the job, they are not likely to rock the boat, break the rules or disrespect authority. They were brought up during wartime, so a "command and control" approach comes naturally.

Characteristics:
- Grew up too young to serve in World War II, too old to be free-spirited hippies who appreciated Woodstock.

- Previously successful at business or raising a family and not ready to really retire.
- See this as time of life to do whatever they want.
- Fascinated by all the life choices available today.
- Formerly conformist thinkers, but have become more daring with age.

Baby Boom Generation (approximately 1946 to 1963)

As products of "The Wonder Years," Baby Boomers were influenced by the indulgence of Beaver Cleaver, the can-do optimism of John F. Kennedy and the hope of the post-World War II American dream. The intense social and political upheaval of Vietnam, assassinations and civil rights led them to rebel against conformity and to carve out a perfectionist lifestyle based on personal values and spiritual growth. They welcome team-based work, especially as an anti-authoritarian declaration to "The Silents" ahead of them, but they can become very political when their turf is threatened.

Characteristics:
- Have the stability and the safety of family and money, love, education and a bright future.
- Know they are to make a difference.
- Have a mission, a purpose and a drive.
- Work together and draw great strength from their unity.
- Do not conform and are not afraid to speak out and be heard.
- Are in search of self, wanting to know "Who am I?"
- Want personal choice and personal power.
- Have rebelled against authority structures in order to gain the authority for themselves for personal expression.

Generation X (approximately 1964 to 1979)

This group is characterized by an economic and psychological survivor mentality. Gen-Xers grew up very quickly amid rising divorce rates, violence and low expectations. Many of them were latchkey children whose parents were not home to greet them after school, so they were labeled at-risk and denounced as slackers. Their youthful promiscuity was stifled by fear of AIDS and warnings that they could die from having sex. They entered the job market in the wake of the Boomers, only to be confronted with new terms like "downsizing" as the economy plunged into recession. They tend to be skeptical toward authority and cautious in their commitments. Their self-reliance has led them, in unprecedented numbers, to embrace "free agency" over company loyalty. Ambitious and independent, they're now striving to balance the competing demands of work, family and personal life.

Characteristics
- Less driven by money than by quality of life and balance.
- Mindful of how workaholism affected their own upbringing. Have seen the damaging effects of their parents' blind loyalty to an organization and aren't apt to share that mindset. Instead, they're loyal to their direct supervisor and their co-workers.
- Have spurred the world's search for true meaning and value in life.
- Love the Earth and fear its demise.
- Expect immediate and ongoing feedback, and are equally comfortable giving feedback to others.
- Value multicultural settings, fun in the workplace and a pragmatic approach to getting things done.
- Viral networkers who consider connecting with people an important task.

- Dislike authority and rigid work requirements, preferring hands-off mentoring.
- Work best when they're given the desired outcome and then turned loose to figure out how to achieve it.
- Sometimes suffer from low self-esteem and don't know where they belong.
- Can be pessimistic and see change and destruction as a way of life.
- Entrepreneurial thinkers.

Y Generation (approximately 1980 to 1999)

Sometimes called the Millennial or Net-Gen Generation, this group contains what were the once ubiquitous "babies on board," the beneficiaries of a backlash against hands-off parenting and a cultural elevation of stay-at-home moms. Coddled and confident, they have a collective sense of optimism, tenacity and heroic spirit, traits sure to be reinforced by the national unity following the tragedy of September 11, 2001. Coming of age during a shift toward virtue and values, they're attracted to organizations whose missions speak to a purpose greater than a bottom line. They're technologically savvy with a positive, can-do attitude that says, "I'm here to make a difference." And they will.

Characteristics

- Extreme innovators but need a team and structure in order to create.
- Won't tolerate anything that's not fast, efficient, new or different enough.
- Believe they know who they are and what they're doing because they have technology and information, even if they lack personal experience.

- Possess great self-esteem and self-worth as well as a strong ego, but not street smarts.
- Practice racial, cultural, religious and spiritual diversity.
- Consider themselves the center of their world.
- Have an opinion about everything and are active globally.
- Seek happiness, pleasure and joy, and believe they can be, have and do anything.
- Overstimulated by activities and technology, which has left them less time to develop their social skills. Tend to be weak in relationships that require intuition, sensitivity and intimacy.
- Want to start at the top. The bottom does not interest them.

New Millennial Generation
(approximately 2000 to present)

Sometimes called The Next Silent Generation, this group's contribution has yet to be determined. There are high hopes the people in this generation will advance the human cause of consciousness. They have a momentous task to set the world right. These are the children of the Generation Xers, picking up the sensitive human nature of their parents.

Characteristics
- More intuitive and creative than older generations were at their age.
- Take to computers like a fish takes to water, with a natural understanding of technology in general that can border on the uncanny.
- Natural healers.
- Know who they are.
- Understand the spiritual beyond their years and have a matter-of-fact attitude toward the paranormal.

- Possess an expanded consciousness infused and expressed through the newest technology.
- Highly sensitive and psychic, and born with important life purposes.
- Stir the interest of many people throughout the world who are watching the profound change in consciousness being manifest in these children.
- Considered an integral part of the positive transformational shift of the new millennium.

EACH GENERATION'S ROLE

No matter how we're labeled or categorized by our external activities and judged by our behaviors or beliefs, there's more going on behind our day-to-day existence. We are working together to unfold and manifest a global purpose. No single generation can do this monumental task alone. Each generation weaves into the next and expresses a piece of the whole.

Each generation carries characteristics that are hidden beneath the surface and not as publicly known. They're not necessarily useful for consumer and political studies, but they're integral to the global sense of purpose. They involve the way each asks and answers the foundational questions of "Who am I?" "Why am I here?" "What is the meaning of life?" and "How can I be of greater value?"

I have added new names for each generation to better match its role in the search for purpose. Think of it as each living two realities simultaneously – the conscious, which was described above, and the unconscious. You could also describe it as the intentional and the unintentional. To know each generation's role, and to know your own part in the search for purpose, you should understand what drives each team unconsciously.

The Silent Generation = The Parents

This is the generation that puts boundaries and limitations around things, instilling control and discipline to foster safety and to build moral character. The people in this group are all about rules, regulations, laws, morals and principles. The safety of the boundaries provides an opportunity for creative expansion. These people act as the parents of the entire community in the search for global purpose. They keep everything in order and reduce the negative consequences of the unexpected. They have a clear understanding about right and wrong – it's black and white with no gray area – and have enforced it and taken responsibility for it. They want to be the best contributor to society.

Primary role in global purpose: To create stability, safety and a strong foundation for building a new world.

Contributions deliberate or intentional: Their traditional and serious way of living. They have put a moral structure in place. They're hands-on, responsible, principled and all about obligations to community – including nationalism, educational institutions, philanthropic organizations and places of worship. They stabilized the foundation by supporting it. This generation went beyond the survival mode of the generation before it, which had lived through the Depression.

Attitudes toward global purpose: As a generation, they have been focused on family, community and nation, not on global purpose. They're just now starting to think about exploring themselves and having fun. They're excited about their grandchildren and great-grandchildren and what they will accomplish.

Other characteristics: This generation is known for its longevity. The reason they're still here is to guide the other generations onto the right path. Once they feel secure their children, grandchildren and great-grandchildren are on their way to global purpose, their job is finished and they can start having fun.

- Responsible for establishing institutions in education, government and social programs.
- Hyper-responsible in their communities.
- Self is not the center – it's community and family.
- Take rules and laws very seriously and put their power in external authorities.
- Respect authority and don't question it.

The Baby Boomers = The Vision Holders

These are the people who hold the seed of human consciousness expansion. They were born knowing there was a global purpose, although not consciously. Their goal is to be "the best I can be." Once they discover who they are, they understand the vision their generation holds and they make it their mission to ensure that vision is manifested. Unlike their parents, they question the status quo. They like to break the boundaries and open the world inside and out. They have looked to both external and internal resources to do this – starting with abstract thinking, which was external, and then turning to internal resources such as Eastern philosophies including Buddhism and transcendental meditation.

Primary role in global purpose: To find themselves, to answer the question "Who am I?"

Contributions deliberate or intentional: They love – not specifically, but globally. They wanted everyone to love, and they were misunderstood by those outside their generation, who called them dreamers and said they were chasing a fantasy. They seek change and justice – not in institutions necessarily, but in humanity as a whole. They love the concepts of freedom, peace and equality because they are part of the vision, but their life goal is to try to bring those to the world.

Attitudes toward global purpose: They have always wanted to break out of the identity and expectations their parents had set and define themselves as individuals. As part of their mission, they support personal choice, which can be seen as selfish by other generations. Vision Holders see personal choice as something critical that's earned when they take personal responsibility for life circumstances. This marks the first movement toward individual self. They were individuals but unified with the rest of their generation as one. They define themselves in relationship to a planet, or the universe, rather than a community or a religious group. They see themselves as a human species rather than a nation.

Other characteristics: The Vision Holders had the stability of the Parents generation behind them, providing safety, family, money and education, taking them out of survival mode. With this firm foundation, they were willing to take risks. They were free to become creative, daring to dream and question. This generation is mischaracterized as rebellious when, in fact, it was curious and focused on expansion of the mind and a passion for speaking out, being heard and shifting the power from external authority figures to individuals. People in this generation didn't need to conform when they were growing up because they felt safe and comfortable with who they were. They were able to take authority back and put it into their own hands. They were the first empowered generation. They have an unconscious, unified mission that started to take shape in the 1960s with Woodstock and war protests. Their sense of purpose lies in a mission to create global community and family.

- Spiritually restless, with shifting alliances and the continual search for something else, a personally authentic spiritual experience.
- Not quite sure how to raise their kids because they're so busy searching for themselves, finding nothing that satisfies or fulfills the hunger for knowing self, which must come before understanding the unified vision.
- Experiencing a combination of spiritual quest and spiritual homelessness.
- Value experience over belief or tradition, stress self-fulfillment over self-denial, and demand tolerance.
- Interested in holistic practices derived from Eastern and indigenous religions that try to link body and soul, including the ecological relationship between humans and the rest of the Earth's body.

Generation X = Meaning Seekers

People in this group want to make a difference in the world. This generation has searched through spirituality and all the alternative forms of religion and expression. This is the first generation to name itself spiritual as opposed to religious. They don't care who they are;

they want to know why they're here. What's the value? They're in the middle of the global change and they feel like they have no power. Constant change is imposed on them, and they're the smallest generation, so they don't have the great numbers like the Vision Holders to make things happen. They love people. They want relationships, love and connectedness. They're viral marketers and networkers. They want community. Beneath the surface, they are somewhat angry. They grew up as latch-key kids, left on their own while their parents worked. They feel the freedom their hippie parents gave them robbed them of structure, safety and a sense of belonging. They choose friendships and relationships over money. They choose quality of life over quantity of life. The back-to-nature movement has come out of this generation, as well as a move to get one parent back into the home to bring up the children.

Primary role in global purpose: Bringing spirituality and connectedness into relationships. Soul mate and soul partnership relationships have come out of this generation. They have accelerated communication, adopting e-mail and cell phones as ways of staying connected with the world.

Contributions deliberate or intentional: They prefer sharing with and helping each other. They prefer living in a small team or small community environment, which replaces the family life they feel they missed growing up. They coined the idea of a circle of friends as their family instead of their biological relatives. They spearheaded the advent of dining out all the time instead of eating at home and hanging out in coffee shops. This lets them gather with their community and friends. They've pushed intuition as an important part of communication and are very in touch with their emotions and sensitivity. They look at spirituality as a way to be closer to self, which lets them be closer to others.

Attitudes toward the global purpose: They are huge environmentalists. They are extremely concerned about the well-being of the planet. They started the animal rights movement. They care about plant life and water and air.

Other characteristics: In reaction to the Vision Holders, they are extremely pragmatic. They don't want woo-woo quackery. They don't want the dream and the fantasy. They want solutions, usable in daily life. They don't use spirituality as inspiration, they use it as a way of living. It has to be attached first to people and relationships and then a measurable outcome or result. They're grounded spiritualists. Instead of running off to join the Peace Corps like their parents, they earn money and donate it to make a difference.

- Tend to be pessimistic to balance the overly optimistic Vision Holders.
- Love to do things that matter to other people.
- Embrace self-less service and humanitarianism.
- Considered a minority because their generation is so small.
- Seek recognition and meaning. They want to make a big splash to make a difference – looking to role models Bono, Oprah, Leonardo DiCaprio, Brad Pitt, Angelina Jolie and Bill and Melinda Gates, who are becoming known for making contributions to world causes.

Generation Y = Techno-Junkies

The children of the Vision Holders, they have been given everything – love, financial security, technology. They've been told since the day they were born that they can do anything or be anything – you name it, it's yours. They're happy and confident. They have a power center different from that of the other generations. Their power comes from their experience and their knowledge of technology. Some learned how to speak, read and write when they were 4. Children of the early Meaning Seekers are also in this category, and not all of them have everything their peers have. So there is a big difference between the haves and the have nots – and all meet in the middle in technology. Instead of being connected to their emotions and feelings like Meaning Seekers, they're overstimulated by technology, which gives them easy access to the left and right sides of their brains, making them action takers and innovators. They want things immediately and thrive on instant gratification. Their main goal in life is to get big money. They want the biggest, most technologically advanced and fastest products.

Primary role in global purpose: As change agents, accelerating change and advancing and driving technology. They are the largest generation since the Vision Holders, and they're conscious, discerning consumers. They want the flavor of the week in new technology – not just once a year at their birthday or Christmas. They're advancing technology all over the globe, which means they're fueling global economic change, flattening the socioeconomic structure. They're doing it through economics, not through human contact. They believe anyone anywhere can be a millionaire. Kids all over the world share this vision.

Contributions deliberate or intentional: Rather than dreamers, these are sharp, clean thinkers and doers. They don't get distracted by dreams. The overstimulation in their environment – with the TV, cell phone, e-mail, instant messaging and iPod running all at the same time – allows them to tune everything out. They can hold focus like no other generation. They turned their weaknesses into strengths very early in life. In fact, they mature very quickly, some starting corporations by age 12.

Attitudes toward global purpose: They're not focused on connecting with people. They take that for granted and believe everyone is equal globally. They live this belief – in their world, all races, cultures and religions are on the same level. They're confident, but they're clueless without a computer or another electronic device. They believe in action and solution, not complaining, whining or being a victim.

Other characteristics: They love to interact via machine rather than in person. They're not as attuned to intimacy and feelings. They have taken the idea of entrepreneurialism to the next level. They are excited about the world. They feel powerful and they know they're going to change the world. They're so savvy about products that they're socially conscious consumers and will choose purchases based on whether they help or hurt the planet.

Millenials = Human Angels

Within the last decade, a growing number of children have been born who appear to be more intuitive and more creative than older generations were at that age. These bright, gifted youngsters were dubbed "Millennium Children" in the book of the same name by Caryl Dennis and Parker Whitman, published in 1998.

Discussed in books or New Age circles, these children represent humankind's best, its hope at the turn of the century as we face both a spiritual and historical crossroads. Sometimes called the "Human Angels," they have the technical experience of the Techo-Junkies generation before them, but they also come equipped with expanded human abilities not seen in any of the recent generations. Their abilities go beyond spirituality into the paranormal and metaphysical.

Human Angels are often the offspring of New Age parents and were exposed to New Age thinking at an early age. Instead of learning just the basics of reading, writing, arithmetic and languages, they're being tested on their psychic abilities. They're being introduced before birth to things like awareness of past lives; empathy with all creatures – not just humans, but animals and plants; communication with the unseen world, including spirits and angels; and multi-dimensional healing abilities.

These children are born with an advantage: They have parents and grandparents who are interested in their advanced human ability so they consciously or unconsciously activate it. It's like learning a different language – if it's a part of their environment at or before birth, they will pick it up easily and with all of the nuances integrated at an early age.

Primary role in global purpose: Extremely bright, quick children with an extraordinary memory and a strong understanding of how the universe works, these are sensitive, gifted souls with an evolved consciousness who have come here to help change the vibrations of our lives and create one planet and one species. They are our bridge to the future. These are the ones the Vision Holders have been waiting for, who can carry out the vision. They have the ability to use the powers of the human soul combined with technology. They are the living form of the vision.

Contributions deliberate or intentional: From the day they're born, they already know how to use the powers of their soul. They don't have to wonder whether those powers exist, or try to connect with them, as generations before them have done. These people were born with the switch turned on, and their parents and grandparents are working to make sure it stays on – unlike in history, when children were discouraged from using soul powers.

Attitudes toward the global purpose: Because this generation is so young, it's hard to know exactly what attitude they will develop as a team. But they're expected to have a global impact. They are called the children who are one. They live total equality and oneness. Dividers and boundaries in humanity drop away, and they see themselves as part of a unit that works together, just as the Boomers did. The Boomers' vision was connected to fantasy; this generation's is connected to reality.

Other characteristics: The Y Generation was encouraged that they can be anything they want to be. This generation is already beyond that – their parents and grandparents look at them with awe. They can't be taught because they were already born wise. Instead, their parents play a support role in helping these children develop. The Boomers expected Gen-Xers to be this way but see now that this is the generation that completes the team.

TYING IT ALL TOGETHER

Now that we know all the teams, their positions, their strengths and their contributions to the vision, let's put it all together. How does one generation in its strengths, weaknesses and interests support the next?

Remember, all of us are living in dual realities that sometimes seem in opposition to each other. That's what creates the whole conflict in the search for purpose.

First let's accept that everyone has an integral role. Each of us is an expert because we exist. There is no single right way anymore. One size will not fit us all. The explosion of creativity and expression has opened a new door of existence in our lives on the planet.

For the fulfillment of purpose to be carried out, we need a director, someone who holds the vision and shows the others how to carry it forward. We need someone who holds the roadmap, the DNA, the whole picture. The Baby Boomers are the Vision Holders. Their time is now.

The Vision Holders are showing signs of desperation because they feel empty, unfulfilled, and that they're not doing what they feel they're here to do. They're getting older and feeling the urgency that their job won't be done. They see the state of the world, with war in many parts of the planet, and they want to resume the momentum they had in the 1980s when the Berlin Wall came down.

We've had a pullback in the past seven years, since the turn of the century. People are bringing their focus back to the vision, to the greater purpose of their existence.

People of the Parents Generation are now letting go, realizing they accomplished their piece of the mission. They nurtured the next generations by providing stability, safety and a firm base for launching the search for purpose.

The Vision Holders are on the threshold of carrying out the manifestation of greater purpose. They have the teams in place and available. All of the team members, even the young Human Angels, are doing their part. The Vision Holders' next job is to reveal the vision, bringing it into the consciousness of the other generations so they can participate on their own terms.

WE ARE ALL PART OF ONE WORLD, ONE MORAL UNIVERSE, SHARING ONE OXYGEN TANK.

– BONO

ENLIGHTENED COMMUNICATION IS COMMUNICATION BEYOND EGO. IT'S A WINDOW INTO A COMPLETELY NEW ORDER OF HUMAN RELATIONSHIP IN WHICH WE NOT ONLY AWAKEN TO A HIGHER STATE OF CONSCIOUSNESS TOGETHER BUT, EVEN MORE IMPORTANTLY, BEGIN TO ENGAGE WITH IT IN ORDER TO FIND OUT HOW TO CREATE THE FUTURE.

– ANDREW COHEN

A PROBLEM CANNOT BE SOLVED WITH THE SAME CONSCIOUSNESS THAT CREATED IT.

– ALBERT EINSTEIN

CHAPTER 5

THE TASK: GLOBAL CONSCIOUSNESS

How do you think people find their purpose?

As long as there is war, disease, destruction, starvation and imbalance, we have not succeeded in our vision and purpose. As long as we have not developed the technology, the science, and our human potential enough to move these things out of our creation and reality, we have not succeeded, we are not finished, we cannot leave.

As long as the power and the potential of the human heart and soul are hidden and closed, and all living things are not treated with honor and consideration of their right to coexist in harmony and joy, and as long as we harbor slavery, hatred and power over others, there is still work to be done. Until the human life experience is one of abundance, wholeness and freedom to create, we have not yet unlocked the human spirit to thrive in its expression on this planet. The most basic of all human needs must be met for all of humanity, not just an individual, family, community or nation.

Until we take the responsibility to communicate in a way that all living things can understand, we are not finished. We must move our collective consciousness forward, out of the fight for survival, out of a place of lack and into the support of creation and abundance. Until we can proudly, without an inkling of shame, pass the torch of life to our great global Millennial generation, we are not there yet. We can't stop the drive that's fueled deep within us to anchor a consciousness that will ensure there's an equal place for all who inhabit the earth.

MULTIPLE LAYERS OF CONSCIOUSNESS

The challenge is to make things that are on our mind now happen before the mind shifts its attention to the next thing, leaving the last one incomplete if it did not happen according to plan in the moment we wanted it.

For each of us, global consciousness presents itself in layers that unfold and grow organically, not consecutively or hierarchically. The layers of consciousness have distinct characteristics that interface energetically with one another:

- Mastery of daily life – often referred to as surviving the mundane. We never really seem to get a handle on the daily interruptions, tasks and emergencies that weigh us down. It seems to be life's mission to manage us instead of us managing life.
- Self-development and personal freedom – a lifetime exploration never completed. This is an ongoing discovery process. As we complete a step, the next one magically presents itself during this profoundly empowering inner journey.
- The leap of human evolution – being pushed at you from all directions, it's hard to keep up with because you have no time to master it or become fluent in it. Human evolution requires other people's resources, so it's always outside your

control and influence, which makes it a source of constant dependence and vulnerability for you.

- Co-creation of the global vision – the process of building the layers into a planetary landscape that interfaces with all living things. Individuals feel clueless about the overall plan, yet they must hold the vision and trust that it's happening even though they have no power, control or authority over it.

Let's explore each layer individually. By understanding more about these and the way they interact with one another, you can begin to see why we sometimes feel as if we're stuck instead of moving forward.

Layer 1: Mastery of daily life

The nature of human life is undirected, without clear boundaries or instructions. It's like the human mind – all over the place, chasing whatever catches its attention or crosses its path, like a child with a butterfly. That's why the squeaky wheel is the one that gets our attention. It's the nature of our human makeup. Where the focus goes, so goes the action. This is a basic principle of manifestation.

So you can see why it's difficult to predict life's path. It doesn't go in a straight line. It flows to and fro, all over the river, as circumstance moves it. Developing mastery is the art of using our internal rudder, skillfully steering our mind, emotions and life circumstances that are bombarded by demands on our attention every moment of the day.

Because we're bound by the non-renewable and finite resource of time, at the end of the day you're grateful to have made it through another 24 hours. But what did you do? Where did it go?

Days move into weeks, gobbled up by doing what has to be done, never being finished, marked by moments of carefully orchestrated "mini-breakouts" that provide a taste of value, meaning and fulfillment to the mundane.

Mastery is not a control over life but a willingness to see it and experience it as it is and then work with it in harmony and in step with it. Accepting and allowing take the push, compulsion, panic and depression out of it. Allowing releases the energy consumed by resistance and protection. It lets you take down your guard and give up the fear that this unruly life will take you over. It lets you release the feeling that if you stop doing what must be done, everything will come tumbling down or, worse, if you don't take care of it now, there will be that much more to do later.

Mastery allows you to flow with what is, and then you can see more of what lies beyond the constant barrages of life circumstance.

Balancing life is a skill. It takes attention, focus and practice. It requires planning, commitment, time and patience. It's not done in a straight line. Life meanders, full of the unpredictable and the unexpected.

This is a process, and it's something we manage and attend to for a whole lifetime, but it's only a small piece of life that we're learning to master. There is more, much more, we must embrace and take action on if we are to fulfill the vision of human evolution.

Layer 2: Self-development and personal freedom

If you would be a real seeker after truth, it is necessary that at least once in your life, you doubt, as far as possible, all things.

– Rene Descartes

Our freedom motivates us to pursue our dreams, passions and happiness, or abundance and the good life. Freedom, self-responsibility, personal choice and expression come out of our exploration and discovery of who we are. The doors of real joy, love and happiness open. You can do or be anything. The possibilities are endless.

We can manifest our dreams, follow our passion, and help to transform the world in crisis. Our level of participation with the planet is changing from passive giving and a feeling of support and helping to being more sophisticated in our assessment of the circumstances surrounding others' life situations.

As you come to know who you are, and are empowered by that knowing, you take a more self-responsible stance in your interaction with others, helping them find the power to change their lives rather than simply handing them a temporary fix. Remember that old Chinese proverb: Give a man a fish and you feed him for a day. Teach a man to fish and you feed him for a lifetime. When The Parents Generation was growing up, the federal welfare system was designed to help get people back on their feet so they could support their families again. It has since become the source of entitlements, carrying people through life for sometimes multiple generations. There's a growing backlash against this today, a desire to get back to helping people help themselves.

As we claim who we are and empower our personal truth, and learn to express outwardly what we have discovered, we become more and do more, not just make more to give more.

Passive giving is not enough today. Anyone can donate money. It doesn't take any real contribution from your consciousness. It's not enough. You must give of yourself – who you have found yourself to be. You are what is needed – your consciousness, your experience, your higher being, the brilliant light of your possibility. Not simply money.

The power of ancient wisdom unconsciously drives us toward our greater being, new creation and alternative expression. When the global vision is fulfilled, and everyone has enough of everything, what then? What will your contribution to your planet be? Our vision calls us to be more, greater, more empowered, more conscious and creative than we have ever been in the past.

Money and things are important to provide a stable foundation in which to take the risk to explore more. These things in themselves fulfill a part of the human longing to be empowered and in control of our destiny. Things and abundance free our minds and spirit to give and become more willing to reach out to others in kindness, understanding and joy. We naturally move into an entirely different part of our expression of the desire to create.

But our experience in creation is limited and not original or expanded. So we rely on the old standards, donating money to charities, education, disaster relief, victims of catastrophes, the sick, the old and the underprivileged.

We as humans will eventually work in unison to find solutions to problems and build things we never knew were possible. In order to step into real solutions to human pain, suffering and repression, we individually must become more of what we were designed to be – and not as a result of new technology or science, but through the authenticity of our humanness.

Level 3: The leap of human evolution

All truth passes through three stages: first, it is ridiculed; second, it is violently opposed; third, it is accepted as being self-evident.

– Arthur Shopenhauer

Human evolution has become a hot topic. Look at what is presented about human possibility every day in recent pop culture:
- The whole Harry Potter craze, including the books by J.K. Rowling, films, wizarding schools and part of a theme park.
- Television shows that depict everyday people with superhuman traits: *Heroes*, *The 4400*, *Roswell* and others.
- The resurgence of traditional popular superheroes, including Spiderman, Superman and Batman.
- Books, films and videos that help people understand the metaphysical: *The Celestine Prophecy*, *Way of the Peaceful Warrior*, *What the Bleep Do We Know* and *The Secret*.

Our daily experience now includes subjects that used to be discussed only as strange phenomena or miracles: higher consciousness, quantum physics, the universe, the light, light-workers, enlightenment, awakening, shamanism, mysticism. These concepts express what's happening in the layers of our vision. Pop culture is bringing them to light, acknowledging what we know of a greater truth and universe.

Communication is taking a whole new dimension as people create new words and concepts, mixing technology and the growing consciousness to implant them into the human psyche. What would people have thought in the 1970s if they'd heard someone talk about Googling, instant messaging or texting another person?

Knowledge of human possibility has been available on Earth throughout this entire civilization. It's been given voice, uncovered and covered up, and hidden over and over again until it was time to be embraced. The covering and hiding is not a conspiracy. Our human possibility is available to anyone, anytime, anywhere. But it's human nature to question, and even reject, things we can't see.

When was the last time you contemplated or were confronted with the concepts of manipulating time and space, understanding frequency and energy fields, bi-location, invisibility, immortality, simultaneous lifetimes, accessing other dimensions and realities? Or the implications of the modern sciences such as genetics, quantum physics, astrophysics and neuroscience? These topics have come to be known as the new sciences of life, the emerging sciences and the advanced energy sciences, or the law of the universe.

These tools and concepts are alive and well, with accounts of everyday people developing and using them. But it takes a quantum leap to observe and accept how nature behaves instead of clinging to the preconceptions of how nature "ought to behave."

Until we put our focus and power into expanding our ability as much as we expand our technology, we will not learn how to use these tools that lie dormant in all of us. Those who do hone them will be accused of being superhuman or even aliens, as they are in the TV shows.

Children's stories tell the story of the awesome and the miraculous, and they do it all without math. The only math that ever can explain a rag turning into a beautiful gown is quantum mechanics. There is a math for that explanation as well as for a pumpkin into a carriage. Quantum mechanics says that the molecular structures that make up a pumpkin also have a potential to be a carriage. All we have to do is change the intent, dissolve the pumpkin and change its intent.

– Ramtha

There are documented accounts of people turning dirty water into wine, or one grain of wheat into enough to feed a village. If we can teach children to be terrorists, we can teach them to disappear, move through time and space, live on air or regenerate a limb. We simply need to make development of our "superhuman" powers as much a priority as we do technology and other education. Reading, writing and arithmetic are the basics and are rapidly becoming outdated. You can excel, contribute and be healthy, wealthy and happy whether you can read and write or not. Our technology takes care of a lot of those basics.

We all have the ability to use our mind to move objects, connect with another person with the heart and soul, pick up the information from a book by putting it under our pillow, or create a parking place when we need one.

To develop any skill, you need to focus your attention on it. If you're overwhelmed in your survival and daily maintenance, or lost in the chaos of your mind not knowing who or what you are, and not embracing your potential or possibility, you can't be more.

The pioneering spirit of the human being, the desire for more, the curiosity, is what brings this knowledge forward again and again. The more people are introduced to it, the more recognized it becomes.

Layer 4: Co-creation of the global vision
What distinguishes this purpose from any other purpose that drives a person? The collective vision – the sheer magnitude of the impact. I'm talking about one of the greatest visions we've ever experienced as human beings in this civilization.

No one group or person can claim this global task. We are our mission. Therefore, to express who we are individually based on an inner knowing and personal awareness, we are driven to a united purpose. This task gives us a platform for grander, more expansive expression.

The goal is unspoken, with no single leader, no apparent rules, and no visible boundaries, yet we know it. The movement is a shared internal force coming from every conceivable direction in every possible expression of humanity. This is how consciousness speaks and guides. It moves silently from soul to soul, connecting, collaborating and communicating nonverbally yet clearly, reaching the parts of us that are listening and ready to hear.

How can we prove it? What evidence do we have that this type of guidance system can exist? How can it be measured? It doesn't matter to us; we do not have to wait for a consensus, agreement or permission to express what we are here to express and to do, what we have to do. We do not have to convince those who don't know or even care.
– Stephen BE of Being There Enlightenment Systems Inc.

So if you can create joy, love and peace, get on with it. If you can learn to fly, pass through time and space, have the love of your life, or be happy, make it happen. Do it for those who can't, who have situations and circumstances that make it so difficult that they're expressing another aspect of human existence, living in Level 1 in survival mode. They do what they can do, so don't judge it or compete with what is not for you to experience. Do your very best to be all you can be. Encourage your children and their children to explore and create. Do your part within yourself. Start learning. Reach out and ask. Forget about what you can't do.

UNCOVERING THE VISION IN EACH OF US

We don't have to have other people's authority or power to validate who and what we are and what we are about. We are what we are, and we're here to live it without apologizing for what we know. This is a vision driven by heart and soul. The instructions are buried in our individual subconscious. It's whole, passionate and inclusive.

We know the peace and harmony that this vision embodies. That is the beauty and the power of it. The vision moves quietly and purposefully undetected below the interference and chatter of the mind, but it is not silent. Its power is far reaching and its impact unmistakable. It is a force that is feared and its value has been recognized.
– Stephen BE of Being There Enlightenment Systems Inc.

The Information Age has ignited our need for knowledge and answers. It has brought an awakening of spirit that was the missing link in our human capacity.

So many people have been on a spiritual journey, an awakening, that it has led us here. Recovery and integration of spirit is a part of the vision. It tells us that when the spiritual movement has come and gone, the purpose will grow stronger within everyone who embodies the seeds of the vision.

Spirituality is becoming more prominent, but the essence behind it has always been there. You either are or are not in touch with that aspect of your human self.

The mind is the mind, the body is the body, and no one is perfect. Neither is the human spirit that expresses itself through our imperfections. They just are. Claim them and they are available to use as tools when you create.

Don't get stuck in perfection here with thoughts of enlightenment or ascension or godlike qualities. Just embrace that you are it, you have it, and you can in time know how to express with it. The awareness of our body, mind and spirit makes the instrument complete. Now we've laid the groundwork for fulfilling our purpose.

THE TASK

The task is to know the vision so fully that we can hold it and talk about it, which will start moving it forward. We need a road map, a manual for carrying out this mission. It will act as a business plan, defining everyone's roles and projecting what will happen, how and when.

Silence is no longer a choice. All of us must find a way to speak our vision and know that's the purpose that drives us. Responding to the drive takes extraordinary courage right now, but as each person finds his or her voice, others will hear and find the strength they need to do what they must do and be who they must be.

The human species is in crisis. The seeds of survival reach beyond the survival of the physical species and into the premise of the survival of a greater consciousness and expansion not yet experienced in this civilization.

The civilizations that have called this planet home before us have revealed themselves to be part of cycles of intelligence that repeat themselves. This is not the first time this cycle of purpose and growth has existed on the planet. There is growing evidence that great advanced societies have expressed themselves on this same ground.

However, this is the first time in our civilization that this explosion in consciousness has coincided with a surge in technology, which gives us the tools for every human being to participate in this creation.

Not being able to manifest the unknown purpose results in a frustration that causes adverse human actions and reactions. This is how we get hatred, war, terrorism. It's OK. We have not lost our way. We aren't sidetracked. We're just cleaning up along the way, ferreting out the conflict, confusions and longstanding disagreements and the fear and pain of growth and change.

This is a global effort, and it takes enormous organization. We've seen other global causes before, and some still continuing: to protect the environment, cure AIDS, eliminate substandard housing and starvation, resolve conflict between nations, and push for world peace. We do have the capacity to work together.

H<small>OW DO YOU GET TO KNOW YOURSELF</small>? I<small>N THE SAME WAY</small>
<small>AS YOU GET TO KNOW OTHERS</small>. B<small>Y SPENDING TIME WITH</small>
<small>YOURSELF.</small>

– K<small>ENNETH</small> M<small>EADOWS</small>

I<small>T STARTED WITH PROFOUND FLASHES OF INTUITION AND</small>
<small>SURGES OF SYNCHRONICITY…AND THESE INTUITIONS AND</small>
<small>SYNCHRONICITIES SWITCHED ON PERMANENTLY AND</small>
<small>NEVER TURNED OFF</small> – <small>NOW THE CONDUIT IS ALWAYS OPEN.</small>

– S<small>TEVE</small> P<small>AVLINA</small>

I <small>DIED A MINERAL AND BECAME A PLANT.</small> I <small>DIED A PLANT</small>
<small>AND ROSE AN ANIMAL.</small> I <small>DIED AN ANIMAL AND</small> I <small>WAS MAN.</small>
W<small>HY SHOULD</small> I <small>FEAR</small>? W<small>HEN WAS</small> I <small>LESS BY DYING?</small>

– J<small>ALAL</small>-U<small>DDIN</small> R<small>UMI</small>

CHAPTER 6

PERSONAL CONSCIOUSNESS

Are you able to articulate your purpose with anyone else?

Our global purpose is to expand consciousness. Let's talk about what that means, why it's important, how it feels, and what expanded consciousness looks like.

As our consciousness grows, we stop being small and our world actually feels like we've been liberated from deep sleep. As our awareness of self expands in our environment, we find ways to understand and communicate in our diverse world.

Expanding your consciousness doesn't mean you have to change or give up anything. It's in your control. It doesn't make you alone or weird and banished from the community. It won't make you lose your job and become homeless and hungry.

Instead, expanding your consciousness is about education, a series of learning opportunities, an exploration just like any pursuit. It will cause you to be scared and uncomfortable at times, but that's small compared with the disappointment, illness and unhappiness that result if you don't pay attention and wake up.

It's up to you what you want to pursue. To expand your consciousness, you have to be open to hearing, seeing, feeling, touching and sensing more profoundly than you have asked yourself to before. It takes courage, intention and commitment. It means you have to reject the urge to go back to a small, comfortable existence that lets you go back to sleep and blame the world for being what it is.

When we experience the ecstasy and purity of awakened human possibility and potential, we know this is everything, and that we've truly discovered what we were seeking. This is the ultimate in expanding.

Expanded consciousness

Consciousness is a state of being. The primary characteristic accredited to it is the ability to perceive life in a more comprehensive way. Consciousness involves interacting with your environment through a heightened state of awareness of yourself and your relationship with your surroundings.

Expanded consciousness is also called higher consciousness, super-consciousness, Buddhic consciousness, objective consciousness, Christ consciousness, universal consciousness, quantum consciousness and God consciousness in various traditions of spiritual science and psychology. The concept denotes the consciousness of a human being who has reached a higher level of evolutionary development and has come to know reality as it is.

Expanded consciousness is an evolution that occurs when spiritual knowledge is applied to the conduct of human life, awakening and developing faculties that otherwise lie dormant in the ordinary human being.

Expanding Your Consciousness

Our consciousness opens to a path that leads us to discover and explore more of who and what people are designed to be. Humans have an extraordinary, complex composition we've only begun to understand.

Life does little to show us how to develop our consciousness. We aren't taught how to make the biggest decisions of our lives, how to cultivate a burning desire for what we want, how to concentrate and set intentions, what power we have when we connect with our inner truth and wisdom, how to develop our intuition, or what to do with the synchronicities that present themselves to us in answer to our need for purpose. But over the course of our lifetime, these skills prove far more significant than anything we learned in school.

Consciousness raising can go in a thousand directions. You can expand your consciousness in understanding the universe, enlightenment, higher intelligence, outer space, the human body, the mind, nature, spirit. The possibilities are infinite.

In this book, we're narrowing our focus to explore expanded consciousness as it relates to the global purpose and the advancement of human impact on our planet.

Expanding consciousness has a lot to do with opening your mind, abstract thinking, moving from what you've known as possible into the impossible. It's about stretching beyond the habitual and routine. It requires an active mind that looks beyond the customary, that questions why and how things are done. The mind that's open and alive is turned on by learning and curious about the universe.

When we're in a setting like a university, we're encouraged to expand our minds, stretching the possibilities of what we can be. What happens to the mind when we step outside that safe environment that supports expansive, abstract thinking, that pushes back against limitations, social guidelines and corporate culture? What happens to the mind when it goes from open and curious to closed and protective?

We go back to a safe, narrow, linear way of thinking, one that complies with authority and is afraid to think out of the box. This way of thinking was portrayed in modern films *The Truman Show* and *The Stepford Wives*. That way of life is not going to work anymore.

A growing entrepreneurial mindset has reopened doors that let us venture from the mainstream in thinking about how we approach life. And the New Age mindset that became popular in the past two decades introduced fringe populations that led us into extreme exploration of consciousness. These two movements are converging in a new way, showing us there are no limits to what the human mind can do. Anything is possible.

This new way of looking at things shows up in our popular culture in TV shows such as *Survivor, American Idol* and *American Inventor.*

Each of us comes here on assignment, and as we pull this understanding into consciousness, we are introduced to the vision of what we want to accomplish with our lives.

We look for a common world vision of how we will all work together to create an expanded global consciousness. The challenge is to hold this vision with intention and focus every day.

This vision represents the creation of a new planetary plan that replaces a 500-year-old preoccupation with survival and comfort. As awareness grows, we open to the reality of a greater purpose of human life on this planet, and an expanded understanding of the nature of our universe.

In order to begin to approach world peace, understanding or even a conversation, we must stand on a broader base of connection and communication. We have to get past our fear of people who are different from us.

The world is diverse. In order to communicate, we need to have more universal understanding and more universal terms. We need to draw from common experiences.

Communication is hard enough among different generations, family members and personalities, let alone people with other skin colors, races, religions, languages, nationalities and political positions. The process becomes complicated. We have trouble getting past the hellos, so how can we reach a level of complex thought and understanding?

HOW EXPANSION OF HUMAN CONSCIOUSNESS AFFECTS YOU

Raising your consciousness is the most powerful and beneficial thing you can do for yourself and others. What are the actual benefits? What makes it so valuable and important to the global purpose? And what does it feel like to expand your consciousness?

Developing your consciousness enhances your self-esteem, deepens your ability to love and be loved, strengthens your self-worth, and raises your energy and your vibration.

You are liberating the miraculous power of human consciousness. And it demands that more and more of us be able to recognize the vastness of the global vision in which we find ourselves, and be willing to take responsibility for its implications.

Expanding consciousness results in a new level of mastering the mind. It makes you a more flexible and agile decision-maker and helps you maintain a steady, positive emotional response regardless of the situation.

Putting your enlightened consciousness to work in your life is the fuel that supercharges your empowerment and enhances your skill to negotiate life and keep your desires and intentions on track. You automatically know what it is to allow, witness, be present, stay balanced and open your heart. Your life exists in the center of what is called "the big picture," making it easier for you to use your natural creativity.

Basic foundations

There are specific and simple ways to engage and expand your consciousness, and they accelerate your experience of life. They include knowing and expressing your personal truth, finding the courage to be who and what you are, pursuing your desire, focusing through a clear intention, and maintaining a healthy body and positive attitude.

Associating with other conscious people helps you sustain the benefits of raised consciousness and encourages you to explore even further.

But first, here are some basics about building your individual focus to fulfill the greater global purpose. When everyone understands these elements, we will have the foundation for humanity to grow into its greatness:

Self-awareness in your surroundings

As you become more conscious, your senses seem to wake up and your awareness of your surroundings explodes. Your attention is drawn more acutely to smells, your taste is enhanced, colors appear more vibrant, and sound seems clearer and more distinct. Your surroundings seem to be enhanced in every way.

One of my friends had always lived by the ocean, but once her senses were awakened, she suddenly noticed dolphins playing in the water, the blue of the sky, the light playing off the sand. Those things had been there all along, but she hadn't noticed them or experienced them to such a degree.

Waking up to your consciousness for the first time is shocking. Everything appears vibrant, and it hits you in your heart, leaving you awestruck. You feel as if your soul has awakened.

You see things as if you're looking at them through different eyes, hearing things through different ears. You might fall in love with your spouse all over again, look at your children with new wonder, find revitalized enthusiasm at work, and feel fresh appreciation for your home and how it comforts you.

As you expand your consciousness, you'll experience periods of confusion when you're ready to take the next "quantum leap" in front of you. This is when your whole reality makes very little sense to you, and you become uncertain of everything. The old patterns are being scrambled to make way for the new.

Once you complete one of these leaps, you enter a period of incredible clarity. Everything in your life starts to make sense on a whole new level.

Health and wellness

As you're working on your awareness, you'll find that your physical wellness naturally surfaces as a priority. The interest in supporting your physical health will seem to come out of nowhere, and with this attention you draw to you the resources you need to develop a more aware and conscious relationship with what you eat and how you exercise, and you move into a preventive approach to maintain your personal vitality.

This expanded personal awareness of your physical health puts you in the driver's seat. Your awareness triggers an expanded confidence about what works for you when it comes to your body. You no longer are dependent on the advice given to you by doctors. You step into a place of self-responsibility that better ensures your health regime is tailored to your needs and not lumped into the formula used on anyone who comes through the door with similar symptoms.

You will find the health formula that's right for you. Your physical vitality is crucial because it's the foundation on which you build your expansion of consciousness. Without a healthy, vital body, you're distracted and pulled away from a greater consciousness that is available to you.

Self-responsibility

Do you trust yourself? What level of responsibility are you comfortable with? Are you confident enough to tackle a grand purpose, or do you stick with the day-to-day challenges?

As your consciousness expands, you'll begin to believe you can handle more meaningful responsibilities. One of the key components of self-responsibility and self-trust is that you no longer can be a victim or blame anyone but yourself for the outcome or impact your belief has on yourself or others. The drive toward purpose is about truth and wholeness and a completely different way of responding to everything. In seeking experiences that lead you to claim more of your personal truth, you increase the speed of your growth into higher consciousness.

Prosperity and success

Expanding and stabilizing your financial position in your life can be directly associated with your consciousness. By making the enjoyment of personal wealth and abundance a priority in your daily awareness, you activate the expansion of your consciousness in this area of your life expression.

By daily focusing your thoughts on what you want, you energize the magnet that attracts the object of your focus to you more readily. You begin to program your mind to work automatically toward your financial goals. As your financial position expands, so do the opportunities for others. This is one of the brilliant benefits of functioning from a more conscious position. As you grow, so do others. Like begins to attract like. Your consciousness is directly reflected to you by your interactions and associations with others.

The more we stay connected, the more we are acutely aware of those times when we lose connection, usually when we are under stress. In these times, we can see our own particular way of stealing energy from others. Once our manipulations are brought to personal awareness, our connection becomes more constant and we can discover our own growth path in life, and our spiritual mission – the personal way we can contribute to the world.

– *James Redfield in The Celestine Prophecy*

Self-empowered relationships

Inner peace, the feeling of centeredness, is a natural outcome of expanding your consciousness. Your life will take on an ease and flow. The bumps and struggles seem to smooth out and your life feels like it becomes your own. Your enhanced personal awareness helps you not only to navigate your daily life more effectively and pleasurably, but also to relate in a more fulfilling way with others.

When you're in this place, there's no room for jealousy or blame. You're completely self-confident, so you're not worried about competing with other people for someone else's affection or a job or a bigger house or a better car. You no longer worry about whether you could be more, better or greater than you are right now. You don't feel a need to play victim.

Instead, you realize you're already living in your magnificence. When you do catch stray ugly thoughts intruding into your mind, you stop and ask yourself, "Does this response or confrontation reflect my magnificence?" If it doesn't, you take a moment and realize you've made yourself smaller than you are, and you choose instead to stand in your power.

Higher part of self

As your basic five-sensory awareness improves, your sixth sense will begin to develop as well. Initially, this might take the form of enhanced intuition. You'll start noticing your gut feeling become more accurate, which will encourage you to pay more attention to it.

As you continue on this path, you might experience occasional flickers of your latent psychic abilities. Perhaps you have a premonition about the future that turns out to be accurate.

Or you have an irreconcilable explosion of highly improbable synchronicities one day. Or you experience your first (probably terrifying) astral projection.

These things might feel odd to you at first because you've never experienced them before. They offer you new opportunities for expanding not only your consciousness but also your human abilities.

Keep in mind that people around you might not experience the same things you do, so they might not relate with your new direction. They might question you or not believe what you're going through until they can see it with their own eyes. You might find it better to keep these things to yourself, or share them only with people who've also experienced them, until they feel strong enough to become your personal truth and you no longer need someone else's validation.

Depending on your previous beliefs, you might need to do some soul-searching to decide whether you want to cling to your old beliefs or update them to be able to take fuller advantage of your new abilities. If you wish to progress in this area, be open-minded in your explorations, but don't be so gullible as to blindly swallow others' ideas without careful consideration.

Connection with a higher spirit

If you already have a relationship with a higher power, such as God or Buddha, expanding your consciousness helps you develop that relationship further.

Spirit is a window into a completely new order of human relationship in which we not only awaken to this higher level of consciousness together but, even more importantly, begin to engage with it in order to find out how to create the future.

Master teachers, gurus, mentors and coaches are powerful and inspiring. They make sure you stay on track and keep you going when you hit a wall or you encounter areas of exploration or discovery that overwhelm or confuse you.

Stepping into a higher level of development takes courage and support, and it's helpful to have someone beside you who has been there already, cheering you on and encouraging your next step. It's very difficult to make lifestyle changes and truly transform your way of being. When the road gets rough, or the way is unclear, we're much more likely to turn away as our willpower fades.

Spirit is an expression of the evolutionary impulse in consciousness, which is impersonal and universal. When awareness, due to ignorance, is trapped in daily life's minutiae by fears and desires, it's impossible to experience the peace, bliss, fullness, ecstatic life-affirming passion of Spirit.

Raised vibration and energy

Another byproduct of advanced consciousness is an increase in your personal vibration and energy. Things come to you with ease. You just think of something and it's there. This feels like magic. Synchronicities appear all the time. You feel like you're on the right path because things happen when you want them to, sort of like a request and a response.

This raised vibration and energy come especially when you apply them to compassion and desire. These are the request part of the equation. The universe seems to naturally respond. Some people call this the Law of Attraction.

Compassion – Compassion is the root of unconditional love, a feeling of connectedness with everything that exists. When you're compassionate, you feel more connected with nature, your pets, even strangers. You might want to reach out and hug a tree.

Desire – When you get clear about what you want, such as by creating an intention, you expand your consciousness. Your mind becomes clearer and more focused. It opens the door for your greater wisdom and intelligence to begin to work for you in your life.

Expansion of human consciousness is everyone's responsibility. In the next chapter, we'll explore how you can apply your own expanded consciousness in your daily life on the way to contributing to the global effort with others.

I UNDERSTAND NOW THAT THE VULNERABILITY I'VE ALWAYS
FELT IS THE GREATEST STRENGTH A PERSON CAN HAVE.

– ELIZABETH SHUE

THIS ABOVE ALL: TO THINE OWN SELF BE TRUE.

– WILLIAM SHAKESPEARE

I ACT FREELY WHEN I AM TUNED IN, CENTERED AND
LOVING. BUT IF POSSIBLE, I AVOID ACTING WHEN I AM
EMOTIONALLY UPSET AND DEPRIVING MYSELF OF THE
WISDOM THAT FLOWS FROM LOVE AND EXPANDED
CONSCIOUSNESS.

– KEN KEYES JR.

CHAPTER 7

GETTING INTO THE DRIVER'S SEAT

Do you think there's a formula for finding purpose?

In order to live a life of expanded consciousness, it's necessary to be in the driver's seat, where you can recognize and live your personal truth. This provides the road map to your destination. Without this point of reference, you'll live your life unable to chart a clear path to your purpose. It's like finding your way without a map, Mapquest.com or a GPS device. You can get there, but it can be a struggle.

Even worse, some of us put someone else's destination into our GPS and then wonder why we end up at the wrong place. Instead, we should use other people's expertise and wisdom as guideposts, motivation, springboards, stimulators or triggers that launch us into our own deeper knowing. Their guidance helps us explore our own wisdom but can't be substituted for our personal truth.

We have an abundance of information available to us from all over the world at the click of a mouse. We gather information and then validate it through personal experience, not based on someone else's expertise or opinion. It's processed through our deepest knowing.

**Information + Personal Experience
= Personal Truth**

**Personal Truth ➡ Understanding,
clarity and life direction**

You might hear someone say something and it hits you in the gut as true or untrue. Or somewhere in the recesses of your mind, you remember or connect with a statement, idea or concept. The thought might run through your mind, "There's something very true for me about that information," or "For some unknown reason, that concept rings true for me." This is personal truth.

The more you're able to speak your personal truth, the more conscious you become. You expand your consciousness by uncovering the things that make you individual. Knowing more about yourself awakens your expressions, perceptions and experiences. It makes you unique.

This sense of knowing is your distinctive contribution to global consciousness. You become your contribution.

MAKING THE CHANGE

Living your personal truth forces you to confront personal choices. This change in you might be difficult to accommodate at first, but the long-term joy of openly living your personal choices based on your truth is worth the short-term discomfort.

It takes courage to make a choice and stand by it when you're faced with resistance and fear from others. Change is not easy for others to accept. Sometimes they never do. Not all the people around you will appreciate your independent expression, especially if they're experiencing you as something different from what they've known you to be.

It might take time before they can move from their resistance to appreciating that your change doesn't threaten them. Ideally, they eventually realize it's an opportunity to experience you in a different way. But remember, how they respond to you is their personal choice as well.

To illustrate this concept, let's look at an example of personal expression:

The food lover who chose health

George loved to eat. He was 50 pounds overweight – a good Italian man with a hearty, healthy appetite. When he turned 40, he decided to become a vegetarian. He had been considering the change for a couple of years and had done his research, so as a gift to himself, he committed one year to explore the impact this change would have on his health, vitality, mental strength and general well-being.

George's mother loved to celebrate, and a 40th birthday was a great reason to throw a big bash. The week before the party, George reminded his family he was a vegetarian and would not be eating meat.

"WHAT?!!" his mother said. "It's your birthday. You have to eat." She ranted on: What could he possibly eat if it was not meat? Then the questions: Is fish meat? Is chicken meat? What's not meat?

Finally, in her exasperation, she said, "I won't have anything to feed you. You'll be sick, and what would the doctor say? I just can't have it this. You must eat!"

George knew he couldn't reason with his mother, so in an effort to help accommodate his personal choice and simple request, he asked her, "Mom would it help if I told you the doctor recommended I become a vegetarian and not eat meat for my high blood pressure and to reduce the risk of heart disease?"

"Oh, my poor baby," she responded. "Why didn't you tell me? I thought this vegetarian thing was just one of those crazy fads you had come up with and you were going to make yourself sick. Don't you worry, I'll let everyone know. We'll take care of you. You won't go hungry. Oh, I know exactly what I'll make."

When George got to the party, the table was covered with vegetarian dishes. All the guests had gone out of their way to accommodate the doctor's orders. George was not surprised, but he was disappointed.

When being a vegetarian was his personal choice, the resistance and negativity from others was fierce. However, if being vegetarian was not in his control – if, in fact, he was a victim to something outside his control, such as health concerns – the attitude was overwhelmingly supportive.

Personal choice takes courage, personal conviction, self-responsibility and fortitude, but it's well worth the effort. The more you exercise it, the easier it gets.

EMPOWERING YOUR INTENDED DESTINATION

Intentions are not about cause and effect. They're about expanding your awareness and raising your consciousness. Setting intention is about exploring possibility without wasting time, energy and effort on starting and stopping.

Kick-start the expansion of your consciousness by using a solid intention such as, "It's my intention to prioritize the growth of my consciousness every day so things magically come into my awareness that inspire me to be more."

Give your intention power by repeating it no fewer than five times a day. Post a copy of it in your bathroom, in your car, on

Expanding your consciousness

- When you've identified people who have already expanded their consciousness, keep up with their dreams and visions, as well as their complaints. Keep up with their language to stay in their communication loop.

- Watch the TV shows and films these others watch, use the technology they use, speak their language, even if it's uncomfortable or unfamiliar to you at first.

- Use their physical tools. Those are full of vibration and information that will help feed your quest to expand your consciousness.

- Don't take it personally if you and your ideas seem not good enough because others have already surpassed you in expanding their consciousness.

- Learn to say yes and hitch your Radio Flyer wagon to their expanding stars and fly with them.

- Don't be judgmental or resistant.

- Stay open-minded and open-hearted.

- Ask for help, whether it's from your kids, other people's kids, teachers, mentors, supervisors, anyone around you.

- Listen a lot and talk less.

- Stay active even if you're tired.

your desk or on your nightstand to make it easier for your mind to stay focused on your destination.

The more you systematically bring your intention into focus, the more things like books, articles, conversations, notices and synchronicities magnify your desire. Signs magically seem to point the way, and your consciousness grows.

Your intention aligns your body, mind and spirit, and allows you to take full responsibility for what manifests in your life. It gives you the power to direct your experience and expression. But there's more than just intention working with you when you focus with clarity and determination on your desire. When you focus, you initiate some Universal Laws of Creating.

Universal Laws

Once you're in the driver's seat, these elements of conscious creating become part of your life:

Allowing – There are all kinds of aspects to this Universal Law, but the one I want to stress here is timing. Keep your eyes open but don't push. Let your actions and plans be inspired. Allow your purpose to unfold. Get out of your own way, and stay in the present. You stop thinking about things as missed opportunities and realize instead the timing wasn't right. Oftentimes we're not aware of other factors that have to be orchestrated, organized and put into place before something can happen. The universe works on its own cycle. In other words, your narrow view of your desire is part of a greater picture, not the center of it.

Practicing the Universal Law of Allowing requires dropping judgment and emotional attachment to what you think is the right way or the only way to manifest your desire. This allows the bigger reality of who you are and the impact your choices make in the world. Manifesting your desires may require special consideration that lies beyond your conscious awareness.

Experiencing The Law of Allowing

Jane put her house on the market February 15 and said she wanted to sell no later than June 15. She had done everything right: staged her house professionally, held agent open houses, made repairs, priced the property correctly and advertised everywhere. She received 10 offers, but all fell apart.

She consulted a psychic, who told her not to be in a hurry. It would be a year before she sold her house. "Yeah, right," she said to herself. "Not if I have anything to do with it. You don't know me. When I set my mind to it, I can do anything."

She buried St. Joseph in the back yard, followed a feng shui chart, baked cookies so their welcoming aroma would fill the house, networked with everyone she knew, contracted with an agent who guaranteed a sale. And still, there was no buyer.

She offered to finance the house so people wouldn't need to put money down. She cleared her own blocks and fears, as well as vacating past spirits from the house. She lowered the price, raised the price, everything possible.

It was now January 3. Jane decided to stop obsessing and pushing. She would allow the house to sell when the time was right for her and the buyer. She had an area picked out where she wanted to move, and her dream house had come and gone twice.

"So there must be a reason and something I'm missing," she thought to herself. On February 15, she went to work and found out her job was to be eliminated in Chicago, but there was a position available in Charlotte, North Carolina, if she would consider it.

Coincidentally, Charlotte was on her list of the top five places she might like to live someday, but she never thought she'd be able to do it. Her best friend had moved there just nine months earlier. Jane loved the weather there. And her company was offering to pay for the move. In fact, her new job would be a promotion – something she hadn't received in four years.

"This is way more than I could have ever dreamed or asked for," she told her friends. "I would've had a new house and been stuck."

Her house sold within two weeks.

Attraction – Just as with The Law of Allowing, there are many facets of this Universal Law, but the one I want to stress here is proximity. One element missing from many people's lives is proximity to the raw materials needed to turn their unique expression into success. People born into "old wealth" families seem to have it all. Part of that comes from being surrounded by constant opportunity. Their world includes the best schools, the safest neighborhoods, the most beautiful surroundings, the finest stores.

Today, telecommunications advances and reality shows such as "American Idol" and "American Inventor" have broken through the barrier of proximity, allowing everyone to access resources and audiences worldwide. Look at how many people have become overnight successes on YouTube.com. People with an internal wealth, such as talent or self-expression, an innovative idea, or a personal insight or truth are now being exposed to people with external wealth, such as money and influence.

We used to try to attract what we wanted by going after it externally – perhaps stretching ourselves thin financially to move to the nicest neighborhood, or working 100 hours a week in the hopes of becoming rich. In recent years, we've shifted focus and are starting to discover ourselves internally, with the goal of attracting our personal version of success in the world.

As a consciousness creator, you have complete freedom to create what you wish through this magnetic process called the Law of Attraction.

Acceptance – We accept that what's in our life in the present is what is meant to be. We're supposed to learn as much from it as we can. Once you take stock of the strengths and weaknesses your limitations and boundaries provide you, then you can work with them and change the way your future unfolds. The world, nature and life give us limitations in order to refine our expression. That's what gives us variety and diversity in creation. This is why people who can't see have ultra-sensitive hearing. Not everyone can be the best at singing or dancing or writing. Everyone has his or her own personal version of "best." It's up to you to find yours.

When you struggle against the nature of what is or who you are, then you're fighting the whole universe. Conscious acceptance gives you the power and strength you need as you consciously manifest your greater purpose.

**Conscious expansion by generation:
What's your role?**

The Parents (born 1930-1945)
Preparing the way for expansion of human consciousness

Vision Holders (born 1946-1963)
Knowing and holding the plan of human consciousness expansion

Meaning Seekers (born 1964-1979)
Relationships of higher purpose to advance human consciousness

Techno-Junkies (born 1980-1999)
Technology that advances human consciousness

Human Angels (born 2000 to present)
Untapped human powers that expand and advance human consciousness

CHANGE THE WAY YOU LOOK AT THINGS AND THE THINGS YOU LOOK AT WILL CHANGE.

– WAYNE DYER

IN THE UNIVERSE, THERE IS AN IMMEASURABLE, INDESCRIBABLE FORCE WHICH SHAMANS CALL INTENT, AND ABSOLUTELY EVERYTHING THAT EXISTS IN THE ENTIRE COSMOS IS ATTACHED TO INTENT BY A CONNECTING LINK.

– CARLOS CASTANEDA

DON'T LET ANYONE TELL YOU THAT YOU CANNOT KNOW THE TRUTH FOR YOURSELF OR THAT YOU CANNOT ACHIEVE YOURSELF SPIRITUALLY WITHOUT BEING TIED TO A TEMPLE OR CHURCH.

– HUA-CHING NI

WE SHAPE CLAY INTO A POT, BUT IT IS THE EMPTINESS INSIDE THAT HOLDS WHATEVER WE WANT. WE WORK WITH BEING, BUT THE NON-BEING IS WHAT WE USE.

– LAO TZU

CHAPTER 8

THE LEAP

What is our responsibility toward manifesting our purpose?

In order for this magnitude of global purpose to be fulfilled, we each need our superhuman self to be at our disposal.

If you are going to be the magnificent person you were born to be, you have to put it in gear now, step into your latent power and move forward.

It's said we use only about 10 percent of our human capabilities. We don't even know it's possible to use the untapped resources of our subconscious mind, so our hidden powers slumber while we go about our daily routines of eating, sleeping, working and plodding through life.

Think what we could be if we took the mystery, miracle and magic out of our potential and started to systematically engage it. We could become capable of extraordinary things.

Listening to a debate about global warming, it occurred to me the conversation is not just about nature but about taking personal responsibility for the impact we have on our planet. It's a desperate cry for expanding our consciousness. Claiming personal responsibility requires you to step into an attitude of personal power, changing your source of power from dependency to self-sufficiency. This stance in life makes way for magnificence to flourish.

You are the master of your destiny. All the power you need lies dormant inside you, hungry for projects to work on, ready to spring into action when you call on it.

But before you can use your expanded superhuman abilities, you must first know you possess them. A worldwide trend toward personal empowerment is teaching us how to draw out the powers of the conscious mind. Today's global communication gives us a wake-up call to show us what's possible. We're hearing about these abilities on the Internet, on television, on the radio, and in books and magazines. Psychologists, metaphysicians, spiritual masters and business leaders all over the world are moving us toward discovering how to use the treasures of the greater human mind.

We're learning to access the power of our conscious and subconscious minds and how to focus on what we want and make it happen, both individually and in teams. We're improving our performance by visualizing each step toward a win or success. We're using mind over matter to overcome obstacles such as physical pain. We're using the power of attraction to draw things and people toward us simply by holding a thought about our desired outcome.

Traditionally, most people are taught to entirely neglect their most abundant source of information, guidance and inspiration by choosing scholarly education and the outer mind, and turning away from the dormant wisdom within them in their subconscious. As a species, we ignore a whole untapped, unexplored human potential.

Our frame of reference of our power comes from our environment: who and what we come into contact with in early life, traditional education, simple life experience, and daily interactions and connections with others. The human being is a sponge and will absorb into its unconscious whatever it's presented with both consciously and unconsciously. That's why kids see things as they really are and can sometimes be brutally honest, and adults have to teach them how society expects them to interpret that reality – hence the phrase "Kids say the darnedest things." How many times have you heard a child say, "Mommy, I can fly!" only to be told to get down from the wall and quit doing something dangerous?

History and research reveal human beings have been so stripped of their powers and the natural ability to adapt, they show signs of being on the verge of extinction.

We can't feed ourselves, fend off disease, or refrain from war, guns and terrorism. We're increasingly susceptible to the forces of nature, including floods, fire, volcanoes, earthquakes, hurricanes and drought.

We've been shown throughout history that these adversities and challenges are not necessary. In the so-called modern world, we're taught to see man's vulnerability. We see ourselves as fragile victims to what we cannot control and have not been taught to manage.

Who is doing this to us? Is it coming from someone's need to enslave parts of the human race in order to serve insatiable greed? Is it a conspiracy?

Or is it natural evolution? Is it truly innocence and naiveté or blatant control and manipulation of the frail human mind and emotions that makes us unable to use our latent abilities to survive, let alone flourish?

The truth is, we've done this to ourselves. We've lost the knowledge about our human potential that's now being revealed and explored.

If we spent as much time and focus polishing our superhuman

skills as we do watching TV or playing on the computer, or even learning how to be afraid of the skills themselves, the development of the human body and mind would begin to be expressed in its magnificence.

If we're using only 10 percent of our brain's ability, why not 100 percent? What are we waiting for? Who or what must give us permission? Someday, expressing our human skills will be in fashion, and we will stand in line to learn how to do it.

SUPERHUMAN ABILITIES

Can you imagine the skills we'll develop as we move into a proactive, creation-based motivation as a way of human expression and living? What could these skills do to expand the consciousness of the planet?

History reveals many examples of how people have overcome adversities and challenges by using expanded human skills: native people who ate the essence of the animal and plants rather than the flesh, and villages that would disappear when an enemy came to threaten them.

There are records of telepathic communication and teleportation among people inhabiting the South Pacific Islands. Reports of children regenerating lost limbs, people walking through fire, people eating poison that passes through the body unaffected.

There are reports of people walking on flood waters and a scout running in the woods and not leaving a single print. Of individuals surviving an avalanche by slowing the heartbeat and breathing to conserve energy to imitate a state of hibernation, or surviving an hour underwater by actually breathing like a fish. Of an entire community fighting off starvation with a single grain of wheat and a will to live. Of using the heat of a person's hands to cook a fish.

These are things from our human history that show us the power and possibility that come with expansion of the conscious and subconscious mind. Think what we could be if we made it part of our basic education system, learned right alongside reading, writing and arithmetic. Think what we could accomplish if we valued our expanded skills the way we do expression of human intelligence in areas such as analysis and philosophy.

If we learned to exercise our conscious and subconscious minds at the same time, we'd develop entirely different skills, along with new ways of expressing ourselves and communicating.

> It is all in human's consciousness. He is limited or unlimited, bound or free, just as he thinks. Do you think that the men you saw walk (on the water) of the stream yesterday to save themselves the inconvenience of this trip are in any way special creations any more that you are? No. they do not have one atom more power than you were created with. They have by the right use of their thoughts forced development of their God-given power. The things you have seen (walking on water, astral projection, healing, levitation, mastery over death, eternal youth) are accomplished fully and freely by you in accord with definite law, and every human being can use the law if he will.
>
> – *Baird Spalding,*
> *Teachings of the Masters of the Far East, Volume 1*

The Conscious Mind

Human beings are born with no outward sign of protection, no shell, poison, quills or colors. Instead, we have weak bodies, tiny little fingernails and toenails, thin hair, skin vulnerable to outer forces such as sun, and minds that are weak and fickle at best. Our species lost its animal instincts and senses long ago. Today, we're dependent in every way on manmade creations, and we rely on our strong, stubborn will along with an overpowering sense of entitlement.

The conscious mind is designed to process what needs to happen now, what has happened in the past, and – based on those things – what could happen in the future.

The conscious mind is well-equipped to review history and make comparisons, to process the functions of speech, movement and body coordination and operate as well as the senses. It's our personal organizer and research analyst. The mind is our quick response system that's always on alert.

Adding high-level complex processing – such as creating something new or innovative from scratch, or holding the same thought in your awareness for minutes, hours or days on end – bogs down the mind's processing system causing a backlog of processing.

Like any slowdown in a system, this backlog takes energy, resources, time and focus away from routine function. Our mind starts to store mounds and mounds of unprocessed information, creating chaos when it comes to analyzing and taking action. We begin to repeat the same mistake over and over in different ways under similar circumstances. You might ask yourself, "I thought I learned that lesson from the past. Why am I doing that again? I thought I'd cleared that out."

When the mind doesn't know what it's basing its decisions and choices on, and the body starts to store the thoughts and emotions as unfinished business, this slows our movement, agility and flexibility. The demand of unprocessed input and outflow encumbers the immune system, causing the whole body, mind and emotional system to be susceptible to disease and dysfunction, depression, indecision, apathy and low energy.

Exploring the human superpowers requires the mind to stay focused for long periods of time. This use of the conscious mind's focus is called manifesting with the mind through intention or attraction. The conscious mind can't provide that level of consistency and accountability. If you use only the conscious mind to attract, it will lose effectiveness as you add more and more tasks.

That's why the process of manifesting is not more widely accepted at this time in human life, where we so depend on the conscious mind as our be-all, end-all resource.

THE SUBCONSCIOUS MIND

Human beings have used mind over matter for self-healing, and science and medicine have gotten involved to help us control the process, making it a dependable resource that can be used on a consistent basis.

But we haven't learned how to control our subconscious mind, our dream center, where we make unusual things happen. This place inside us is reserved for functions outside of our ordinary routine that demand more energy, fuel, time concentration, attention and effort than most of us have. Therefore, we keep looking to science to give us a system, instead of developing this resource inside ourselves.

If we instead shift the time and energy spent in needless worry and protection into creating outside the box, a lot can happen quickly. The subconscious mind is capable of processing enormous amounts of information. It's our onboard computer system.

As long as you're in action, your subconscious mind can receive input and respond unconsciously. That's why they say if you want to get a job done, give it to a busy person and it seems to just fold right into what he or she is already doing.

You give your subconscious mind a task, and it has the use of all resources available to it to get the job processed and organized. All you have to do consciously is take the action needed to manifest it in the physical, such as phone calls, meetings, contacts, scheduling or budgeting. No haphazard, time-consuming scrambling, loss of focus or interruptions. The plan is easy to follow and execute because all of the detail of processing is already done. It's expressed by some as this incredible "mind dump." They put the details and thoughts in place and out comes a completed project all linked together in perfect order with the I's dotted and the T's crossed.

Creating with your subconscious is an altogether different approach to project design, proposing, planning and implementation than you'd use when you're engaging only the conscious mind and your standard resources. Creating with the subconscious mind is a developed skill, not magic. Some people have stumbled on the system quite innocently and are considered advanced or genius-level thinkers. They see themselves simply doing what seems logical or natural to them.

It's through the use of the subconscious mind that mountains can be moved. This is a powerful internal teamwork and partnership everyone can access. It's no more difficult than brushing your teeth. And in time, it gets that automatic.

Our subconscious mind loves things to do. It sits dormant in rest mode most of the time because we never ask it to do anything. When we're just navigating everyday, mundane life, we have very little use for this power system – much like those who buy the latest computer system and use it only to send and receive e-mail.

The subconscious mind gathers information and processes it based on the project assigned. So you want to create a new widget? Give the plan to the subconscious mind, which will process it instantly.

Innovators and inventors, some of our greatest thinkers and leaders, have tapped into their subconscious mind.

This mechanism inside us can process hundreds of projects at a time. It's not limited to the linear processing of the conscious mind. You can't overwhelm the subconscious. It's hungry for assignments. The more you give it, the more it thrives.

Creation that comes out of our subconscious is inspirational and moves our heart and soul. All truly great people instinctively have drawn from this rich place within themselves, applying the most basic of human powers without always having been taught how to use them.

It's the subconscious mind, not the conscious one, that serves as the control center for the superpowers.

Conscious mind vs. subconscious mind

The conscious mind handles everyday tasks and decisions. The subconscious mind handles larger-scale issues that call for greater clarity and have an impact on others. Many times, we feel we don't have time for issues that require quiet contemplation, and these are ones we can hand over to our subconscious mind, which doesn't compete with chaos. Oftentimes you feel impatient right before you hand over an issue to your subconscious mind because you haven't been able to get to it with your conscious mind.

Conscious mind
- Grocery list
- To-do list
- Daily chores and responsibilities
- Everyday decisions
- Keeping on track and organized

Subconscious mind
- Emptiness and lack of fulfillment
- Big dreams, big ideas and innovation
- Inspiration
- Personal crisis
- Major decisions requiring clarity and direction

SPECIAL POWERS

I wanted to find out how some people use superhuman powers that are learned in life through trial and error but aren't necessarily taught and passed down from generation to generation. I sent out a questionnaire to a select group with the following questions:

Have you ever discovered you could do things or witnessed things other people weren't able to do or said were not possible? Do you ever use your mind to do things other people say can't be done? How do you use your magic in your life? How did you learn these techniques and how and when do you use them?

No one asked me for clarification. Everyone seemed to understand they do possess powers other people can't see. Their answers were varied, but there is an underlying theme. Here are some of their answers:

"I use the 'teslering' technique from the book *A Wrinkle in Time* to use time efficiently. If it takes three hours to drive somewhere, I know I can do it in an hour and that's what happens – and without me speeding. I learned this from my third-grade teacher."

"I hate to shop, so I use 'expanded seeing,' sometimes known as remote viewing, to browse through a store before I get there. This helps me quickly locate what I'm looking for once I'm inside the store. I learned this from Silva Mind Control."

"When I'm preparing for a meeting, I use a combination of expanded seeing, intention and connection. I visualize the people I'm meeting with and have a conversation with each of them ahead of time in my mind to set the agenda. This allows me to connect with everyone before I get there and helps make the meeting more efficient. Everyone is on the same page before the meeting gets started. I call this my pre-negotiation process."

"Before I travel, I use my 'pink bubble' technique to imagine a protective shield around my car. I've taught this to my entire family."

"I visualize myself arriving safely at my destination, and then I'm not worried when I'm traveling."

"When I was 5 years old, I learned from a children's cartoon how to breathe underwater through my invisible gills. To my mother's horror, I tried it out when I was swimming in the local quarry at age 6. It was quite successful, by the way. I was underwater for about 10 minutes."

"I visualize a sphere or white cocoon to protect me before I go to sleep. A good friend taught me this."

"When I'm confronted with a particular situation or experience, I try to remember I have a choice in it all. I can be reactive and emotional or I can be present in it all and follow what comes to me in the moment."

"I get what I want when I know what I want and don't waffle. Many years ago, I saw my mother wearing some very pretty but discreet diamond earrings. I said, 'I want some diamond earrings, but I want a carat for each ear and I don't want to have to pay for them.' I now have my dream earrings. The first one came as a ring my stepfather gave me. The second one came three years later from my real father. I got several jobs and cars and places to live with that same formula. Set it and forget it. But when I waffle, that is quite another story."

"When I feel overwhelmed with no spare time, I visualize a tube on top of my head. I visualize all I need to accomplish going up the tube and then coming down the tube finished. I do this daily for many of the things I need to take care of, big or small. Things get done very efficiently."

"I bend time by asking it to get me downtown in time for an appointment, even if I have limited time to get there. I always make it, then I thank time for doing that."

"If I'm feeling a bit chubby, I tell myself before I go to bed that I will be thinner in the morning and that my jeans will be a bit looser on me. I sometimes even say what I will weigh. It almost always works. I lost one pound since yesterday morning."

I was born in a small rural town in Ohio where most people shared the vision of what life was supposed to be: family, community and hard work. Yet my early childhood orientation set the stage for my quest to meet individuals who exhibited amazing abilities and to verify that we, as human beings, are capable of far greater achievements than is commonly believed and that the capacity of the human mind has yet to be tapped.

From the time I was conceived, my mother would read to me from *The Life and Teachings of the Masters of the Far East* by Baird T. Spalding, a five-volume series about a scientific expedition of 11 men who visited the Far East in 1894. The research team released its report after spending 3 years living in the remote regions of the Himalayas among extraordinary human beings who exhibited phenomenal paranormal abilities: teleportation, psychokinesis, levitation, clairvoyance, remote viewing, invisibility, extrasensory perception, and regeneration. These were normal daily phenomena in the Himalayan people's lives.

My mother's curiosity led her to read everything she could find that explored human possibility inside and out. She took my siblings and me to visit an African bushman elder. We spoke with an older philosopher at the library. We visited a medium to look deeper into our universe. We received items in the mail from the Theosophical Society in England. She was fascinated with anything theosophical, metaphysical or even extraterrestrial.

Over the years, I've been fortunate to witness extraordinary human abilities and have discovered some of my own. I've adapted them and use them in my life as I need them. Through my work, I help others do the same.

I have personally witnessed teleportation, walking through walls, walking on water and fire, materializing physical objects,

117

instantaneous healing, regeneration of a limb, turning water into wine, a single grain of wheat made into a loaf of bread, objects moved with the mind, perfect and exact telepathic thought transference, complete disappearance, flying, and the list goes on and on.

These are considered superhuman abilities or what I call superpowers reserved for few people – maybe just those in comic books – but they're real. These powers lie dormant inside each of us. Just as some people are more talented at singing, dancing, solving math problems or fixing computers, we all have the potential to specialize in abilities that currently seem beyond our grasp.

STEP INTO YOUR SHOES

Are you aware of your power? Can you honestly say that you are genuinely aware of who you are? Do you see yourself as a vital, unstoppable, person who gets what you want? Are you happy with the life you've created? And if not, do you realize you have the power in your hands to change it when you so choose? Do you know yourself as the gifted human being you were meant to be?

The key to fulfilling your purpose is in knowing who you are and living up to that image.

When was the last time you re-evaluated the image of yourself you hold in your subconscious mind? Was it during your adolescence? In your 30s? On your 50th birthday? When you retired?

In most cases we make small insignificant adjustments to our self-identity as we pass through life, but not enough to really change our belief in who we are or have become. Yet we continue to develop through education, experience and wisdom. Meanwhile, stirring within us are the seeds of who we've come to this time in life to be.

In order to fulfill a global purpose, you need to embody and reflect this magnificent truth about you as a human being as your birthright and as your DNA code. Update your awareness of your creative potential. Fire the old image and look in the mirror at who you truly are and who you know yourself to be. Recovering your greatness requires an updating of your attitude toward yourself and the world.

Once you know you have access to your subconscious resources through the expanding of your awareness, you'll recognize you own an extraordinary life force and creative potential. This is the ultimate source of your love, money and health. This is your untapped abundance and joy.

Just as you'd take responsibility for your daily roles as child, parent or employee, for instance, and your heath, investments, car, jewelry and the lives of yourself and your children, you need to consider taking responsibility for your power and protecting the latent wealth and potential of your consciousness. Use it wisely, with awareness and clear choice.

If you don't protect and take responsibility for this power source, there are many others who understand its value who are more than happy for you to put it in their charge so they can use it at will.

By considering how much more we are designed to be, we can make the leap into fulfilling our life purpose much more attainable without making it a job. These concepts can lighten up your burden and free you to have some fun.

Remember to include life in the plan. Stop to smell the roses, hug your kids, and enjoy the everyday actions, events and celebrations that embrace the human experience. Remember to factor in life: the births, the weddings, the illnesses, the accidents, the deaths, the acts of nature, the forces of spirit, the stirrings of the human heart and soul, the passions, the disappointments, the bumps in the road and the start-overs.

And remember, being all you can be will stretch you out of your comfort zones of safety. It will take you into the brilliance of possibility that comes with creating. It will wait until you take the time to deal with life. You won't have to worry about missed opportunities. The door is always open.

LIVE YOUR PURPOSE

Expanding your consciousness aligns and prepares you to do everything with greater purpose. Your being becomes your mission. Your thoughts, actions and focus are consciously and unconsciously raising the awareness of the planet and making an impact on the world of the future.

When you have your consciousness open and available to be accessed, you're doing your part. It will all unfold systematically. When you're using your greater awareness, you're making a long-term difference. You're creating value and character. You are changing the planet, and you're operating as an instrument of the highest good.

Don't underestimate the importance of being all you were designed to be and living, expressing and creating from your very core. You are your life purpose. Wake up and take the leap into the greatness you were born to experience. All it takes is you being you and no one else.

Greatness of purpose is no longer the exception reserved for only the very elite, gifted or wealthy. This is for everyone, including not just you but everyone else on the planet. The options and roadmaps are infinite. Now is the time to find your personal way to manifest your part of global purpose, your unique formula to expand your consciousness to its greatness and manifest your piece of the planet's great evolutionary leap in consciousness.

By taking hold of your personal power, re-evaluating and updating what you need for basic protection and safety, learning to create out of pleasure instead of fear or pain, and applying your latent superhuman skill set, you can do what it takes to consciously co-create a new planet and advance the human experience.

Our magnificence is yet to come.

ACKNOWLEDGMENTS

Oscar Lizarazo and his family, who show me by example to live every day from the very heart and soul of my greatest purpose.

Jackie Woolf, for making sure I was not naive and that I kept putting the power and wisdom where it was needed.

My mom, Sarah Haushalter, who tirelessly lives her purpose with grace and fortitude.

Diane Sears, my editor, who, when I threw a tantrum and threatened to abandon this meaningless book, patiently waited for the storm to pass and placed it gently but forcefully back in my lap.

Jill Shargaa, my graphic designer, who made the book real and saw me gasp when I witnessed the power and light it contained.

My sister, Sally Haushalter, who impatiently waited and reminded me the world couldn't wait another 30 years for this book and offered to do anything to make it easier for me to focus on the task – including cutting the grass, cleaning the windows, fixing the roof, anything I used as a distraction.

Robert Autry, my trainer, who weekly demonstrated the power of hanging in and moving through to find my "Tipping Point," the exact effort needed to produce the greatest gain in everything I do.

Pam Williamson, who protected my soft spots, anywhere I was vulnerable.

Sharon Rod, who gave me a purple pen with the power of St. Germaine to help me start writing.

My internal and external associates, who allow me to create with inspired intention and action.

About the Author

Maxine Jones is an author and an international personal and professional coach who specializes in uncovering the power of the soul to develop a person's achievement, fulfillment and heart-centered success. Her life's work is about helping people connect with the deepest part of themselves so they can transcend the ordinary struggle of life and participate in creating a greater world for all of us.

Since 1982, she has worked with individuals as well as large corporations, unlocking that hidden dialogue that changes a person's life forever.

Maxine started her career as a marketing/advertising executive at one of the largest firms in Chicago. In the late 1990s she worked with Fortune 100 companies to research the impact of gender-based physiological differences on organizations, leadership, performance and achievement. Through her seminars and retreats for executive clients, she enabled organizations to improve the contribution of women in the workplace.

She left the corporate world to pursue a career that would better match her dedication to higher education and spirituality. Since then, Maxine has trained people in yoga, massage, health and wellness, and wilderness survival skills. She was appointed to study and teach Native American culture. She was selected as a Fulbright Scholarship candidate to work in secondary education in Tanzania. She participated in Kenya on an ecological initiative with the Smithsonian Institution and also initiated, developed and implemented a humanitarian project in Botswana.

Maxine realized her special intuitive powers when she was a young child and communicated with an imaginary friend she later came to know was her soul. She was raised by two highly educated parents who inspired her to pursue her dreams. Her mother was a theologian, metaphysician and dietitian, and her father was an international transportation engineer. When she was very young, Maxine met an African elder who became her mentor. Meanwhile, she trained for the Junior Olympics in gymnastics. She also earned state championship titles in swimming and diving and became an avid tennis player. Today she is a certified scuba diver.

Maxine is trained in nursing and holds a bachelor of science in psychology and a master's in human resource development and education from DePaul University. She has delivered keynotes and led seminars and retreats on health and psychology to audiences as small as 30 and as large as 1,500. Today she delivers customized presentations, seminars and retreats on the power of the soul.

Want to talk with Maxine?

Visit www.maxinejonesandassociates.com
or call for an appointment
(770) 934-3819

YOUR BEAUTIES, MAGIC AND MAGNIFICENCE FOREVER LIE AS SEEDS ALIVE WITHIN YOU. LET YOUR TEACHERS COME TO YOU; THERE ARE MANY BOTH INSIDE AND OUT. YOUR GREATEST TEACHERS AND LIFETIME PARTNERS COME TO YOU AS UNSEEN FRIENDS WHEN YOU ARE VERY YOUNG. WELCOME THEM AS A VALUABLE PART OF YOURSELF, GIVE THEM PERMISSION TO BE YOUR TEACHER AND FRIEND, TO SHOW YOU THINGS ABOUT THE PERFECTION OF LIFE THAT NO ONE ELSE CAN OR EVER WILL.

– MAXINE JONES

Want more?

Books

Meet Your Soul: Stretch Your Wings and Fly
A Guide to Connecting with Your Power
Learn how and where to find your soul and how to develop a life-changing relationship with this hidden part of yourself.
- Softcover $19.95
- eBook $19.95

Also in the Stretch Your Wings and Fly Collection

Launch Your Inner Radar: Empowering Your Soul
A Guide to Activating Your Life Purpose
Learn how to identify your true self-identity and your life's calling, which allows you to embrace your past, improve your present, and celebrate and explore your future. (Available after 6/08)
- Softcover $19.95 • eBook $19.95

Take the Limits Off Your Power: Freeing Your Hidden Success
A Guide to Feeding Your Hungry Soul
When you allow your soul to be a true partner and friend, your life becomes a profoundly different experience. The connection enables your soul to do everything in its power to support you to find fulfillment in your life. You encounter synchronicity, miracles and unexplained phenomena. You learn to interpret your life as your soul would. (Available after 9/08)
- Softcover $19.95 • eBook $19.95

Soul Relationships: Mates, Partners and Teams
A Guide to Creating a Life with Greater Purpose
Relationships that are motivated by a greater purpose and supported by soul are something many people only dream about. Your soul knows how to make these relationships work and can help you build them. (Available after 2008)
- Softcover $24.95 • eBook $24.95

Audio

Desperately Seeking Purpose: Why Am I Here?
Each Generation's Role in Raising Global Consciousness
- Audio book – Listen to the audio version of the book. Available in CD or MP3 download. $28.95

Meet Your Soul: Stretch Your Wings and Fly
A Guide to Connecting with Your Power
- Audio book – Listen to the audio version of the book with separate meditation CD. Available in CD or MP3 download. $34.95

- Audio of meditations and exercises and includes a workbook. Available in CD or MP3 and e-book download. $24.95

- Audio of meditations only from the book. Available in CD or MP3 download. $14.95

- Self-training course and workbook – Four-CD set of instructions, meditations and exercises to guide you through the process of meeting the soul. Available in CD or MP3 download. $99.95

Discounts are available for quantity orders. Special orders such as excerpts, booklets, workbooks and other products can be created in print or electronic formats to fit your needs. Contact Cherry Tree Publishing at **info@cherrytreepublishing.com**

Speeches and workshops

Maxine Jones is available for speaking engagements and workshops. For a list of suggested topics, please visit **www.maxinejonesandassociates.com**

Order Form

By fax: 770-934-1965 (24 hours a day)

By mail: Cherry Tree Publishing
PO Box 450962
Atlanta, Georgia 31145

By email: info@cherrytreepublishing.com

Please send me:

_____ copies of *Desperately Seeking Purpose: Why Am I Here? Each Generation's Role in Raising Global Consciousness* - $19.95

_____ copies of *Launch Your Inner Radar: Empowering Your Soul A Guide to Activating Your Life Purpose* - $19.95

_____ copies of *Take the Limits Off Your Power: Freeing Your Hidden Success A Guide to Feeding Your Hungry Soul* - $19.95

_____ copies of *Soul Relationships: Mates, Partners and Teams A Guide to Creating a Life with Greater Purpose* - $24.95

Name_____

Address _____

City/State/Zip _____

Sales tax: Please add 7% to the total order for books shipped to Georgia addresses.

Shipping: $4.95 for the first item and $1.00 for each additional item

Payment method: ☐ Check   ☐ Visa   ☐ MasterCard

Card Number _____

Name on Card _____

Expiration date _____

3-digit number on back of card _____

D<small>ESPERATELY</small> S<small>EEKING</small> P<small>URPOSE</small>